NO PLACE LIKE
HOME

NO PLACE LIKE
HOME

STEPHEN CLYBORNE

No Place Like Home

Copyright © 2022 Stephen Clyborne

All Rights Reserved

ISBN 979-8-218-05582-0

Unless otherwise noted, all Scripture quotations are from the New Revised Standard Version Bible: Anglicised Edition, copyright © 1989, 1995 the Division of Christian Education of the National Council of the Churches of Christ in the United States of America. Used by permission. All rights reserved.

Scripture quotations marked KJV are taken from the Holy Bible, King James Version. Public domain.

23 House Publishing
Greenville, South Carolina
PRINTED IN THE UNITED STATES OF AMERICA

Dedicated to my mother,
who never delivered a sermon,
but was the best preacher in our family.

Table of Contents

Preface	ix
Prologue	xi
Acknowledgments	xiii
No Place Like Home	3
The First, the Last, and the Only Questions	9
Accepting, Trusting, and Resting in God's Love	17
Doing What We Have to Do	23
Get Out of the Boat	33
How to Understand the Bible	41
It's Not About You	49
Life Is Hard, But God Is Faithful	57
Making Peace with Our Past and Our Future	67
Somebody's Gotta Go	75
Stand Up Straight	83
The Economy of God	89
The Energy of Righteousness	99
The Long-Awaited Kiss	107
The Path of Peace	115
Walking in the Light That Has Been Given to Us	123
Walking the Fine Line	131
Why the Cover-up Is Worse Than the Crime	139
Why We Love the Lord	147
You Are Here, But So Is God	153
Sing Your Way Home	161

Sermons for Special Occasions

As Slow as Christmas (Advent)	171
Getting the Christmas Story Right (Christmas)	179
He Appeared Also to Me (Easter)	187
The Motherly Love of God (Mother's Day)	195
Outloved by the Father (Father's Day)	203
The Intersection of God and Country (Independence Day)	207
Some Blessings You May Not Have Counted (Thanksgiving)	215
Epilogue	223
Touchstones of My Preaching	231

Preface

The year 2022 is the centennial year of the church I am privileged to serve and is a milestone year for me and my ministry. As of this year, I have served Earle Street Baptist Church in Greenville, South Carolina, for twenty years and have been in full-time, vocational ministry for forty years.

Because my own personal story is intermingled with the history of Earle Street Baptist Church, it was timely for me to offer this book of sermons as a tribute to my heritage of faith and my journey of ministry.

Actually, to tell this story, I have to go back further than a hundred years. On May 7, 1893, Central Baptist Church (originally named Rutherford Street Baptist Church) was constituted with eighty-nine members. Not long after that, the Reverend Dr. J.A. Brown, who was pastor of Central from 1907-1909, was the first to see the need for a church in what he thought of as the "northeastern section of the city." He used the occasion of Central's twentieth anniversary to share his vision of establishing a savings account for that purpose. Central was only twenty years old, and already the vision of establishing another new church was developing. And in 1922, Earle Street Baptist Church was organized with 117 members, eighty-three of whom came from Central. It was in that same year that my own personal connection with Central was established. In the same year when Central began Earle Street, a woman named Margaret Nichols Clyborne, my paternal grandmother, was baptized at Central while she was pregnant with my father. In 1923, my father was born, and was enrolled in the Cradle Roll of Central Baptist Church and remained at Central until Central closed its doors eighty years later.

At the age of twenty-nine, my father was baptized at Central in 1952, the same year he and my mother were married. My mother, who had been a lifelong Methodist, joined Central as well and was baptized there. Later, my two older brothers were baptized there — and in 1969, when I was ten years old, I was baptized there, too. Our roots at Central were deep. Central reached its peak in membership in the 1950s and '60s, and began a gradual decline until 2002, when it voted to close its doors and join Earle Street Baptist Church. The mother church that had given birth to the daughter church was now asking the daughter church to take her in.

It was in that same year, 2002, that I joined the staff of Earle Street Baptist Church as associate pastor. In some ways, it was a sad picture of the decline of my once-thriving home church. But in other ways, it was a beautiful picture of the circle of life — the life of the church and my own personal life coming full circle in 2002. Almost overnight, in addition to finding a new church family at Earle Street, I was reunited with my home church family from Central, worshiping with my own parents and brothers again, as well as with other people from Central who had such a profound impact on my life. Until that time, I had seen God's hand most often in retrospect. But this was one occasion when I was able to trace the hand of God in real time. In 2009, my role at Earle Street shifted from associate pastor to senior pastor, and over the past twenty years, my love for the church has only deepened with each passing year.

As Earle Street Baptist Church prepares for a second century of ministry, these sermons are my way of honoring the spiritual heritage that was passed along to me through my home church, my current church, and the other churches I have been privileged to serve for the past forty years.

Prologue

How does a pastor select a limited number of sermons from forty years of ministry? One way is to choose only those sermons that are worth repeating and reading, which in my case, narrows down the choices considerably. I take great comfort in believing that God has chosen to use "the foolishness of preaching" to communicate the truth of the gospel because that is how I feel about so much of my own preaching. I cannot count the number of times through the years when I preached a sermon that I thought was grossly inadequate, and someone came up to me afterward to tell me how he or she heard the voice of God through it. Sometimes what people hear is not what I thought I said, or intended to say — but still what they needed to hear. There is a mystery to preaching that I cannot explain, and no one else can either. But for the purposes of this book, I wanted to include sermons that represented the major themes of my preaching — themes that are worth repeating, even if the sermons themselves are not.

A criterion I used in selecting the sermons from this book was to gather input from the congregation I have been privileged to serve for the past twenty years. When I asked the church to submit suggestions for the book, I was hoping that some people might remember some of the sermons I have preached, but I was fearful that I might be underwhelmed by the lack of responses. I was prepared to entitle the book *Sermons No One Remembers* — but as usual, the people of our church family were gracious in their responses.

And of course, my poor wife, Sylvia, has earned the right to have special editorial privileges since she has been subjected to my preaching more than anyone else. More about her in the Epilogue.

Acknowledgments

In putting together this book, I am again indebted to Butch Blume, who guided me through the process of writing and publishing my first book, *23: Growing Up in the Space Between Harry and Celeste*. Once again, Butch made it happen. He advised me at every step along the way, designed the book cover, and offered encouragement that kept me moving and focused. Linda Kirkland, a retired English teacher, proofread the book and corrected my many errors. Libby Young, a member of our church and a librarian at Furman University, helped me research a lot of my sources so I could document them properly. All of these people were cherished friends before this process, and are even more special to me now. I could not have completed this project without their help.

NO PLACE LIKE
HOME

No Place Like Home
LUKE 15:11-32

¹¹ *Then Jesus said, "There was a man who had two sons.* ¹² *The younger of them said to his father, 'Father, give me the share of the property that will belong to me.' So he divided his property between them.* ¹³ *A few days later the younger son gathered all he had and traveled to a distant country, and there he squandered his property in dissolute living.* ¹⁴ *When he had spent everything, a severe famine took place throughout that country, and he began to be in need.* ¹⁵ *So he went and hired himself out to one of the citizens of that country, who sent him to his fields to feed the pigs.* ¹⁶ *He would gladly have filled himself with the pods that the pigs were eating; and no one gave him anything.* ¹⁷ *But when he came to himself he said, 'How many of my father's hired hands have bread enough and to spare, but here I am dying of hunger!* ¹⁸ *I will get up and go to my father, and I will say to him, "Father, I have sinned against heaven and before you;* ¹⁹ *I am no longer worthy to be called your son; treat me like one of your hired hands."'* ²⁰ *So he set off and went to his father. But while he was still far off, his father saw him and was filled with compassion — he ran and put his arms around him and kissed him.* ²¹ *Then the son said to him, 'Father, I have sinned against heaven and before you; I am no longer worthy to be called your son.'* ²² *But the father said to his slaves, 'Quickly, bring out a robe — the best one — and put it on him; put a ring on his finger and sandals on his feet.* ²³ *And get*

the fatted calf and kill it, and let us eat and celebrate; [24] *for this son of mine was dead and is alive again; he was lost and is found!' And they began to celebrate.*

[25] *"Now his elder son was in the field; and when he came and approached the house, he heard music and dancing.* [26] *He called one of the slaves and asked what was going on.* [27] *He replied, 'Your brother has come, and your father has killed the fatted calf, because he has got him back safe and sound.'* [28] *Then he became angry and refused to go in. His father came out and began to plead with him.* [29] *But he answered his father, 'Listen! For all these years I have been working like a slave for you, and I have never disobeyed your command; yet you have never given me even a young goat so that I might celebrate with my friends.* [30] *But when this son of yours came back, who has devoured your property with prostitutes, you killed the fatted calf for him!'* [31] *Then the father said to him, 'Son, you are always with me, and all that is mine is yours.* [32] *But we had to celebrate and rejoice, because this brother of yours was dead and has come to life; he was lost and has been found.'"*

Most of us have heard this story of the so-called "prodigal" son, and some of us many times. The word "prodigal" never appears in the story itself. It is just a word that is used to describe the younger son in this story. According to Webster, the word prodigal means "given to extravagant expenditure; lavishly bountiful." And it is easy to see why that word is often used to describe the younger son in this story. After all, he could not even wait for his father to die before he took his share of his father's inheritance, left town and partied it all away. He squandered his father's hard-earned inheritance on wasteful and riotous living. If there were ever a clear-cut case of a low-down, ungrateful son, here it is. "Prodigal" is mild compared to some of the words we might use to describe him.

Once his money was all gone and his options ran out, home started looking better to him. Even his father's servants had it better than he had. So he went home. If he ever wanted to eat something besides pig slop again, he was going to have to swallow his pride, admit he was wrong, endure the self-righteous comments from his brother, and take his chances on going back home. In a pigpen, up to his knees in slop, he learned what some of us still have not learned: that the real party is not out in the fast lane, but at home with the father.

Luke tells us that the reason Jesus told this story in the first place was that the scribes and Pharisees were murmuring because Jesus not only hung around the wrong kind of people, but he actually ate with them: tax collectors, sinners, disreputable people who were not welcome in religious circles. It was one thing for Jesus to speak to these people, but for Him to sit down at the table and actually break bread with them was another thing. It was unacceptable. It was offensive. It was downright disgusting to them.

So instead of arguing with these self-righteous religious leaders, instead of condemning them or even ignoring their charges, Jesus did what He so often did. He told them a story. In fact, He told them three stories, all of which are similar in many ways. The first story was the story of the lost sheep. There were 100 total, and one missing. And the shepherd was not willing to settle for ninety-nine. He searched tirelessly for that lost sheep until he found it. And when he found it, he was so happy and relieved that he threw a party in honor of that lost sheep and invited all his friends and neighbors to celebrate with him. And Jesus said, that is the scene in heaven when just one sinner repents. There is more joy in heaven over one sinner who repents than over ninety-nine so-called "righteous" people who need no repentance.

And just in case the scribes and Pharisees didn't get the point, Jesus told another story. This was a story about a woman who had ten coins that were very valuable to her. She lost one and searched diligently for that lost coin. She swept the dusty floors of her Palestinian house until she found the coin that was missing. And when she found it, she, too, threw a party and celebrated. And Jesus concluded that story the same way He had concluded the first story. It was almost as if He were saying to those self-righteous scribes and Pharisees: "Look, in case you don't get it yet, God is more joyful over just one sinner who is lost and will repent than this woman was who threw a party when she found that valuable coin.

In both of these stories, the emphasis is on joy and extravagance. First the shepherd, then the woman threw a party when that which had been lost was found. It seems a little odd that a shepherd would invite friends and neighbors just because one sheep had been found, and a little strange that a woman would invite friends and neighbors to celebrate with her over finding just one coin that had been lost. But Jesus said, "That is the way God is."

And then, so they could not miss the point, Jesus told this third story, the story we now know as the story of the prodigal son. It is, by far, the most developed story of the three. In this story, rather than the father searching diligently like the shepherd had for the lost sheep and like the woman had for the lost coin, the father waited at home for the lost son to return. It seems that, by telling these stories, Jesus was illustrating two sides of God's nature. God is the kind of God who searches until we are found, but God is also the kind of God who waits for us to come home. In this story, the father was not out searching the highways and hedges for his prodigal son. He was not frantically trailing or following His son like some "helicopter parent." He was home, where he had always been ... waiting. So if we find ourselves separated from God, it is not because God has moved. Sometimes God follows us and searches us out, but sometimes God stays put and patiently waits.

God waits for our sins to run their course. God waits for us to come to our senses. God waits for us to realize the value of home. God waits for us to admit the mistakes we have made. God waits for us to find our way back home. But whether God is out beating the bushes looking for us, or whether God is home waiting for us — whether *God* finds *us* or *we* find *God* — the result is still the same: there is unspeakable, indescribable, extravagant joy.

Rather than giving that wayward, prodigal son what he deserved, the father threw a party in his honor. And it was not a low-key get-together; it was a blow-out! It was as if his son were some kind of hero. He put a ring on his son's finger and a robe on his back, ordered that the fatted calf be killed so that there would be plenty of expensive meat to eat at the party, and called his friends and neighbors to celebrate with him! This was one more party — all because a prodigal son realized the mistakes he had made — all because one of his children had come home. And if the word *prodigal* means "given to extravagant expenditure, lavishly bountiful," then this story leads us to believe that it was actually the father who was prodigal.

As the story ends, the older son comes in after a long day working obediently in the field as he had always done, hears the party going on, but refuses to go in. His argument seems to be a valid one. All these years, he had obeyed all the rules, was squeaky clean, and the father had never thrown a party like this for him. My reaction, to be honest, is the same. This doesn't seem fair! It isn't fair. God is not fair. God is more than fair. God does not give us what we deserve. God gives us more than we deserve. God doesn't deal with us on the basis of merit, but on the basis of grace alone. And we can murmur and complain on the sidelines with the scribes and Pharisees and the older brother and all the other self-righteous religious people, or we can join the party. The same God who searches you out waits for you to come home.

The prodigal son began to realize that home is not ultimately about a place. Home is about a face. Home is where God is. We are never home unless we are with God and God is with us. But if that relationship is in place, anywhere can be home.

Even when our sinful disobedience has led us away from home, God has left the porch light on. He has kept the home fires burning. There is a sense in which God searches for us as that shepherd searched for the one lost sheep. He searches for us as diligently as that woman searched for that valuable coin. But there is a sense in which God waits for us to come home. It is not just that God will *bring* us home; it is that God will *be* our home. And if we will come home, the joyful celebration here will be nothing compared to the joy there will be in heaven. Wherever you are, God will be your home. Whatever you've done, God will forgive.

The picture this parable leaves in our minds is a picture not so much of a place, for the place finally is incidental. It is a picture of a face. The porch light is on. The home fires are burning. Home is where God is. There's no place like home because home is not a place. God will bring you home, and God will be your home. Amen.

The First, the Last, and the Only Questions

GENESIS 3:1-9; 4:1-9

---

¹ Now the serpent was more crafty than any other wild animal that the Lord God had made. He said to the woman, "Did God say, 'You shall not eat from any tree in the garden'?" ² The woman said to the serpent, "We may eat of the fruit of the trees in the garden; ³ but God said, 'You shall not eat of the fruit of the tree that is in the middle of the garden, nor shall you touch it, or you shall die.'" ⁴ But the serpent said to the woman, "You will not die; ⁵ for God knows that when you eat of it your eyes will be opened, and you will be like God, knowing good and evil." ⁶ So when the woman saw that the tree was good for food, and that it was a delight to the eyes, and that the tree was to be desired to make one wise, she took of its fruit and ate; and she also gave some to her husband, who was with her, and he ate. ⁷ Then the eyes of both were opened, and they knew that they were naked; and they sewed fig leaves together and made loincloths for themselves. ⁸ They heard the sound of the Lord God walking in the garden at the time of the evening breeze, and the man and his wife hid themselves from the presence of the Lord God among the trees of the garden. ⁹ But the Lord God called to the man, and said to him, "Where are you?" — Genesis 3:1-9

> *¹ Now the man knew his wife Eve, and she conceived and bore Cain, saying, "I have produced a man with the help of the Lord." ² Next she bore his brother Abel. Now Abel was a keeper of sheep, and Cain a tiller of the ground. ³ In the course of time Cain brought to the Lord an offering of the fruit of the ground, ⁴ and Abel for his part brought of the firstlings of his flock, their fat portions. And the Lord had regard for Abel and his offering, ⁵ but for Cain and his offering he had no regard. So Cain was very angry, and his countenance fell. ⁶ The Lord said to Cain, "Why are you angry, and why has your countenance fallen? ⁷ If you do well, will you not be accepted? And if you do not do well, sin is lurking at the door; its desire is for you, but you must master it." ⁸ Cain said to his brother Abel, "Let us go out to the field." And when they were in the field, Cain rose up against his brother Abel, and killed him. ⁹ Then the Lord said to Cain, "Where is your brother Abel?" He said, "I do not know; am I my brother's keeper?" — Genesis 4:1-9*

There is so much about God we cannot understand. Shrouded in mystery, God is beyond anything we can say or think or imagine. So most of us have more questions than answers about God's nature, God's purposes, and God's ways. We often say, half-jokingly and half-seriously, "If I ever get to heaven, I have some questions I want to have answered." But the Bible is quick to remind us that what matters more in the end are not *our* questions for *God*, but *God's* questions for *us*.

Sometimes our questions can become clever ways of avoiding God's questions. If we can focus on our agenda, somehow we can avoid God's agenda. Many of us take our questions to the Bible, and we should. But not as many of us are as eager to deal with the questions the Bible brings to us. We have been conditioned to believe that there is an answer in the Bible for every question. But it has never occurred to many of us that the

Bible, frankly, doesn't seem to be concerned with many of our questions. And what is even less obvious to many of us is that, as long as we focus on *our* questions, we do not have to come to terms with the questions the Bible raises. Maybe it is time that we come to the Bible to listen not for its answers, but for its questions. Maybe it is time for us to let the Bible set the agenda for us rather than the other way around. The Bible has its own questions for us — and in the end, they are the questions that matter more.

Speaking of questions, the first narratives in the Bible have generated many questions — historical questions, scientific questions, and theological questions. But we often fail to realize that these stories have their own questions of us. They are the first questions from the mouth of God in Scripture, and they may just be the most important and urgent questions we will ever have to answer. These opening chapters of Genesis provide a theological introduction to the rest of the Bible. And as it turns out, once God raises these questions in the beginning, the Bible never changes the subject.

The first question raised by God comes in the context of creation. Most of us are almost too familiar with this story. As we read it, we intuitively sense that it is our story, too — and before we know it, it begins to read us. It is the story of how God created the world and all that is in it. But it was the man and the woman, created in God's own image, around whom the rest of creation was centered. God placed the man and the woman in a garden of Paradise and made just one rule: they should not eat the fruit from the forbidden tree of the knowledge of good and evil. But the serpent planted seeds of doubt not by a temptation to do something vulgar or corrupt, but by the temptation to be like God. It was not a downward call that got them, but the call upward that got them. Are we not supposed to aspire to be like God, to be godly, to be God-like? It seemed to be a noble calling — but they knew as soon as they ate the fruit, that they had broken fellowship with their Creator. The Bible says it this way: "Then the eyes of both were opened, and they knew that they were naked; and they sewed fig leaves together and made loincloths for themselves … the man and his wife hid themselves from the presence of the Lord God among the trees of the garden" (Genesis 3:7-8). If it were not so tragic, it would be comical. In fact, from a distance, there is an amusing quality to the story. But when we get closer to it, we are ensnared by this story as we see ourselves in that same garden, hiding, as it were, from our Creator.

Have you ever tried that — hiding from God? It doesn't work very well, does it? Sometimes we think that, because we have managed not to get caught by someone else, we have hidden from God. So many of us give every appearance of having our lives together. We have made it in the corporate world. We are living in the fast lane. We work so hard to give the impression that our lives are respectable and put together. We may seem successful by the world's standards — but before God, we are naked, exposed. We find our own ways to cover ourselves and our shame by sewing together a few fig leaves. But no matter how clever or elaborate our cover-up schemes may be, there is nothing we can do to hide from God.

Covered with fig leaves and hiding in shame, the man and woman heard the sound of the Lord God walking in the garden in the cool of the day, and they knew they had been caught. The guilt was eating them alive, and they got real quiet. It was the classic case of hide and seek. But this was no game. They were hiding and God was seeking. And in the deafening silence, the Lord asked the question that still rings in our ears: "Where are you?"

Now we presume that the Lord asked that question not because the Lord needed the information. Surely God knew where they were just as much as parents usually know where their young children are hiding. After all, as the story goes, God knew exactly where to find them. But God was asking the question so that they would have to admit where they were.

It was as if God were saying to them, "Just look at you. Take stock of your life. Realize where you are and where your sin has led you. You are naked, ashamed, humiliated, and afraid. You are hiding from the very One who made You. Your sin has broken fellowship with the only One who can save you. I already know where you are. But I want you to see where you are."

It is the first question the Bible ascribes to God. And it may be the most basic, urgent question you will ever hear God ask: "Where are you?" Where are you in relationship to God? Where has your sin led you? Where has your disobedience taken you? Where and why are you hiding? No matter how cleverly you think you have covered your tracks, God sees and God knows — whether anyone else does or not. It is when we come clean before God, and answer that probing question, that restoration and reconciliation can occur. It is not that God needs our confession. It is that we need to admit where we are because, wherever we are, that is where God will meet us, forgive us, and restore us.

Well, that was the first but not the last question God ever asked. In the very next story, the same God who came looking for Adam and Eve, came looking for their son, Cain. You may remember Cain's story, too — a tragic story of petty jealousy which ended in murder. Cain and his brother, Abel, both offered sacrifices to God, who accepted Abel's offering, but not Cain's. Cain let it get to him. Rather than letting it go, he stewed in it. And one day, as he and his brother were out in the field, Cain killed Abel. And the Lord asked yet another probing question: "Where is your brother?" (Genesis 4:9).

Cain replied, "I'm doing well to keep up with myself. Am I supposed to keep up with my brother, too?" Actually, that is my paraphrase. Cain's actual reply was a question that has hung in the air since it was first uttered: "Am I my brother's keeper?" (Genesis 4:9).

The Lord, not to be diverted by Cain's double talk, rephrased the question: "What have you done?" (Genesis 4:10).

Now again we presume that God is asking the question not because God was curious, but because Cain needed to answer. Cain needed to come to terms with his responsibility not just for himself, but for his brother. We have been created by God not just for fellowship with God, but also for fellowship with one another. Yet some people stubbornly refuse to see the connection between God's first question and God's next question. We disregard people on the basis of their race or political persuasion. We disrespect people whose opinions are different from ours. We turn a blind eye to the people right in front of us who desperately need what we could so easily give. We dismiss people who are different from us in a variety of ways. We mistreat people who get in our way. We indulge our petty jealousies and insecurities to make ourselves feel better. But to relate to God as Father is to relate to others as brothers and sisters. We are our brothers' and sisters' keepers. We do have responsibility not just for ourselves, but also for one another. And yet many of us come to church every Sunday holding on to and nurturing bitterness and hatred and resentment. We hide behind the hymns we sing, the smiles we wear, and the prayers we pray. But no matter where we hide and what we do, the question of God seems only to get louder: "Where is your brother? Where is your sister?"

When it comes right down to it, God has only two questions to ask. Oh, they may be phrased in different ways throughout the Bible, but God never gets too far away from these two questions: "Where are you?" and "Where is your brother or sister?" You can read the rest of the Bible, from cover to cover, and never get past those two questions.

When asked about the greatest commandment, Jesus said it this way: "The first is to love God and the second is just like it, love each other" (my paraphrase). And the writer of First John echoed the same truth when he wrote: "Those who say, 'I love God,' and hate their brothers or sisters, are liars" (1 John 4:20a). The world will know we love God not by what we say we believe, but how we love. It is the theme of the Bible, and the agenda of God expressed in the form of two probing questions: "Where are you?" and "Where is your brother or sister?" The Christian faith doesn't get any more basic than that.

In these stories from Genesis, God's disposition toward sinners was expressed in terms of judgment and grace. God did not leave them in their shame. Nor does God leave us in ours. God takes no delight in our failures. God gets no pleasure in condemning our sin. To Adam and Eve, God showed judgment by expelling them from the garden — but God showed grace by sparing their lives and making clothes to protect them as they left the insulated environment of Paradise. And to Cain, God showed judgment by condemning him to a life of wandering — but God showed grace by putting a protective mark on Cain's head so that no one would harm him.

Now we may walk away from these passages as if we never heard those questions. Or we may try to change the subject by asking our own questions of God. Or we may spend our lives feverishly sewing fig leaves together, trying in our own ways to cover our shame and disgrace. But there is nowhere we can go to avoid the penetrating questions of God: "Where are you?" and "Where is your brother or sister?" We can answer those questions now, or we can answer them later. But before we dismiss these questions for now, we would be wise to consider the chilling possibility that the first questions God ever asked may also be the last questions God will ask, and will finally be the only questions that really matter.

Accepting, Trusting, and Resting in God's Love

1 JOHN 4:10-19; JOHN 3:16

¹⁰ In this is love, not that we loved God but that he loved us and sent his Son to be the atoning sacrifice for our sins. ¹¹ Beloved, since God loved us so much, we also ought to love one another. ¹² No one has ever seen God; if we love one another, God lives in us, and his love is perfected in us. ¹³ By this we know that we abide in him and he in us, because he has given us of his Spirit. ¹⁴ And we have seen and do testify that the Father has sent his Son as the Savior of the world. ¹⁵ God abides in those who confess that Jesus is the Son of God, and they abide in God. ¹⁶ So we have known and believe the love that God has for us. God is love, and those who abide in love abide in God, and God abides in them. ¹⁷ Love has been perfected among us in this: that we may have boldness on the day of judgment, because as he is, so are we in this world. ¹⁸ There is no fear in love, but perfect love casts out fear; for fear has to do with punishment, and whoever fears has not reached perfection in love. ¹⁹ We love because he first loved us. — 1 John 4:10-19

¹⁶ For God so loved the world, that he gave his only begotten Son, that whosoever believeth in him should not perish, but have everlasting life. — John 3:16 (KJV)

When I was growing up, and someone did something hateful, Daddy would say, "She is just mean as sin." Mother's view was a little more nuanced. She would say, "Well, Harry, she acts in an unloving way because she does not feel loved." Daddy would say, "No, that's not it. She's just mean as sin." As usual, Mother and Daddy were both right in different ways. Some people are mean as sin. But often beneath their hatefulness is a feeling of never having been loved.

One of the hardest things for some people to believe is that they are loved. That is usually because they do not *feel* loved. You may be one of those people. Maybe the people in your life have conditioned you to *feel* unloved. Somewhere along the way, someone might have hurt you, abused you, or neglected you. Maybe you blame God for all the cruelty you have faced in this life, and you reason that, if God really loved you, God would not have allowed these cruel things to happen. Or maybe you blame yourself for the mess you have made of your life, and you do not feel worthy of anyone's love, especially God's love.

If that is how you feel, then your attempts to love God and others will be limited, distorted, and corrupted. If you feel like God is an enemy whose favor you must win,[1] that love must be *deserved* to be *enjoyed*, then your love for God and others can become unhealthy and impure. But if you can put aside your feelings and believe that God is "a Friend whose love you can trust,"[2] then your love for God and others will be healthier and purer. There is a *lesser* way to love and there is a *greater* way to love.

Jesus taught us that the greatest commandment of all is to love God with all of our heart, soul, mind, and strength. But living "the greater

---

1 Charles E. Poole. *Don't Cry Past Tuesday* (Macon, Georgia: Smyth and Helwys Publishing, Inc., 1991), 22.
2 Ibid.

way" does not begin when we love God. It begins when we fully accept, trust, and rest in God's love for us, whether we happen to feel it or not.

"The greater way" does not begin with us, but with God. "In the beginning, God …" That is how the Bible begins, how the world was created, and how love originated — in the beginning with God, who *is* love. Because God was in the beginning, and God is love, then God's love for us always precedes our love for God or for anyone else.

God *is* love, and God *so* loved … Think about how that famous verse unfolds. God so loved the world that He *gave* … So, love was not a *feeling* as much as it was an action. God loved the world so much that God gave the only, unique, one-of-a-kind Son of God. The love of God was not just some vague sentiment. Love was a sacrificial gift — a gift that was both cosmic and personal. God so loved the cosmos, the world, the entire created order — not just the people in it, but the vast created order that God had spoken into existence. But God's *cosmic* love is so *personal* that it includes *whosoever* (put your name there). Even though God loves the *world*, as Augustine is often quoted, "God loves each one of us as if there were only one of us to love."

John 3:16 continues. God so loved the world that He gave His only begotten Son, that whoever *feels* God's love? No! Whoever *believes* in Him … will have eternal life. Eternal life is not what happens when life *ends*; it is what happens when life *begins*. Whenever we *believe* that God loved us enough to give Jesus for us and to us, whenever we believe that we are loved by God, whether we *feel* loved or not, that is when we really start to live — abundantly and eternally. That is when we come alive. That is when we begin to live and love "the greater way" — the way we have *been* loved by God. Some people wait until they *feel* it to believe it. But the Bible consistently teaches us that we *believe* it first, whether we happen to *feel* it or not. And then the most amazing thing starts to happen. When we *believe* we are loved by God, when we accept God's love, trust God's love expressed in Jesus Christ, and rest in it, then we are set free to love the way we have been loved — "the greater way."

In the broadest of terms, there are only two ways of organizing our lives. We can live in *love* or we can live in *fear*. Some of us live our lives in fear — fear of the future, fear of what others may think of us, fear of what God may do with us, fear of what will happen to us, fear of life, fear of death, fear that we will be found out, fear of rejection, fear of the truth, fear of lies, fear of crime, fear of punishment — on and on the list may go. And if I have not named your fear, then you fill in the blank yourself. Fear has a way of paralyzing us. It places unnecessary restraints on us. It hems us in. It robs us of the joy of living. It causes us to shrink back and hide when we should be living life to the fullest. And it has been that way since the very beginning.

But in the passage we have read today from First John, we are reminded that perfect love — God's love — casts out fear when we accept, trust, and rest in the love of God, who sent Jesus to be the Savior of the world. Perfect love casts out fear when we confess that Jesus is the Son of God. When we abide in God and God abides in us, when we believe that we are loved completely and perfectly, we have nothing to fear — not even the day of judgment. John tells us that we will know that God's love has been perfected in us when we can face the ultimate fear of God's judgment with confidence, fully accepting, trusting, and resting in God's complete, redemptive, powerful love. "Fear," John says, "has to do with punishment" (1 John 4:18). But love has to do with mercy. When we allow ourselves to be fully embraced by God's perfect love, fear will no longer have any power over us, we will love God in return, and we will be set free to love as we were created to love.

So we can, and many people do, love others without loving God first. But "the greater way" to love is to tap into the Source of love. To love "the greater way" is to believe that there is a Love that precedes any love we can generate on our own. In this passage, John tells us that God *is* love, and we love God because God *first* loved us. And then we love each other because we *first* love God.

There is a lesser way to love and there is a greater way to love. "The greater way" begins with the Source of love. God's love for us was first. And God's love for us will be last. And if we can just accept that we are loved by God no matter what, if we can trust that God's love for us in Jesus Christ is real and true, and if we can just rest in God's love without feeling as if we have to earn it, then we will be ready to live and love "the greater way." God's love preceded everything else. It was God's love that spoke this world into existence. My professor at Furman, Theron Price, said it this way:

> God's love will see the world to sleep. In life, it will bear us up. In death, it will pillow our heads in perfect peace. And in the kingdom beyond death, it will disclose in perfections beyond our conceiving, all we have hoped and feared to see.[3]

One of my beloved former pastors, Ansel McGill, was once rebuked by some of his critics for preaching too much about God's love. "It's all you ever talk about," they said. And I remember thinking when I heard about it, "Boy, if I were going to be remembered for preaching about something too much, if I were ever going to be criticized for repeating myself over and over, I hope it will be for that."

Some time ago, I attended a preaching conference. And one of the speakers said something that has stuck with me. He said, "When you are dead or gone, or dead *and* gone, the people you have pastored

---

3 Theron Price. *Faith, Hope, and Love* (a booklet of meditations presented during a retreat at Lake Junaluska, September, 1980).

should be able to agree on what the theme of your ministry has been. They may not like it. They may not agree with it. They may wish it had been something else. But they should be clear about who you were and what you were about. I do not know, and may not want to know, what people might consider to be the theme of my preaching. But I can tell you what I hope they would say. When I am dead or gone, or when I am dead *and* gone, I would want people to know that the theme of my ministry was the theme of the Bible: God's redeeming love.

> *Redeeming love has been my theme, and shall be till I die.*
> *And shall be till I die, and shall be till I die.*
> *Redeeming love has been my theme, and shall be till I die.*[4]

---

4 William Cowper. *There Is A Fountain*. Public domain.

Doing What We Have to Do

1 CORINTHIANS 9:15-23

15 But I have made no use of any of these rights, nor am I writing this so that they may be applied in my case. Indeed, I would rather die than that — no one will deprive me of my ground for boasting! 16 If I proclaim the gospel, this gives me no ground for boasting, for an obligation is laid on me, and woe to me if I do not proclaim the gospel! 17 For if I do this of my own will, I have a reward; but if not of my own will, I am entrusted with a commission. 18 What then is my reward? Just this: that in my proclamation I may make the gospel free of charge, so as not to make full use of my rights in the gospel.

19 For though I am free with respect to all, I have made myself a slave to all, so that I might win more of them. 20 To the Jews I became as a Jew, in order to win Jews. To those under the law I became as one under the law (though I myself am not under the law) so that I might win those under the law. 21 To those outside the law I became as one outside the law (though I am not free from God's law but am under Christ's law) so that I might win those outside the law. 22 To the weak I became weak, so that I might win the weak. I have become all things to all people, that I might by all means save some. 23 I do it all for the sake of the gospel, so that I may share in its blessings.

When I was a young boy, I had these rare moments of rebellion against my father. Now you would have to know my father to understand why these rebellions were so rare and so brief. But there were some memorable occasions when my father would ask me to do something I didn't want to do, and I would ask, "Why?"

He would invariably say, "Because I said so."

And sometimes before I knew what I was saying, I mouthed off, "I don't want to."

But he would always reply, "I didn't ask you if you wanted to." In my family, nothing was up for a vote. There were many occasions when I didn't have a choice. But I learned at an early age that there were some things in life that I had to do whether I felt like doing them or not. And looking back, I realize now that some of the most unselfish and noble things I have ever done were things I would not have chosen to do. I did not feel like doing them, and in some cases I even resented having to do them. But I learned early on that there were some things I had to do, and that lesson has served me well during some of the hardest times of my life.

There are those people who tell me that if my heart is not in what I do, I may as well not do it because, I have been told, if I do something I do not really want to do, I am a hypocrite. I've heard many people use this line of reasoning, and I have used it myself. After all, it does me no good to go to church if my heart isn't in it. Right? I may as well stay at home. And why bother to pray, read the Bible, teach a class, minister to a person in need, witness to an unchurched friend, if my heart is not in it?

Those kinds of questions could legitimately be asked of Paul. Why do you do the things you do? By the time he wrote this letter to the Corinthians, he had been persecuted and driven out of Galatia, opposed and threatened in Iconium, stoned, dragged out of the city and left for dead in Lystra (and that was just on his first mission trip). I'm sure that if

I had encountered that degree of persecution and opposition on my first mission trip, I would not have planned another one any time soon. But Paul did, and his second mission trip wasn't any easier. In Philippi, he was dragged into the city, stripped, beaten with rods and attacked by the crowds. There in Philippi, he was imprisoned and shackled. In Corinth, though he was opposed and reviled, attacked and brought before the tribunal, Luke tells us that "he stayed a year and a half teaching the word of God." Now, sometime around AD 55, some twenty years after his conversion, as he begins his third (and what would be his last) mission trip just a short time after leaving Corinth, he writes back to the church of Corinth to address some of the issues that were dividing that troubled church.

Someone could have legitimately asked, "Why would you put yourself through all this?" Why *did* Paul do the things he did? Some observers and students of Paul have concluded that he was trying to make up for lost time, compensate for his guilt, rise above his own physical challenges (whatever they were), and we might be able to speculate and add our own explanations as to why Paul did what he did. But perhaps the highest, purest, and noblest reason of all was because he knew he had to do it. "An obligation is laid upon me," he wrote to the Corinthians. "Woe to me if I do *not* proclaim the gospel!" (1 Corinthians 9:16).

It is hard to know exactly what to make of that statement. Does that mean that Paul had no choice in the matter, that he was just playing out a predetermined script for his life? Or was it more that he just felt obligated and compelled to do what he did out of a sense of duty?

Have you ever felt that compelled to do something — like you had no choice in the matter? Have you ever felt like you had to do something that you may not have even wanted to do? As I listen to Paul, it seems to me that the reason he did what he did was about more than predestination or duty. It was about his identity. What he *did* grew out of who he *was*. It was inconceivable to Paul that he would consider doing anything else except what God had called and gifted him to do. To fail to do it would amount to a denial of who he was. He was just living out his sense of calling.

In reflecting on his own sense of identity and vocation, Frederick Buechner tells of a time when a woman said to him, "I hear you are entering the ministry. Was it your own idea? Or were you poorly advised?"

Buechner said:

> … the answer she could not have heard even if I had given it was that it was not an idea at all, neither my own or anyone else's. It was a lump in the throat. It was an itching in the feet. It was a stirring in the blood at the sound of rain. It was a sickening in the heart at the sight of misery. It was a clamoring of ghosts. It was a name which, when I wrote it in a dream, I knew it was a name worth dying for, even if I was not brave enough to do the dying myself.[5]

It is not just an idea. It is not necessarily something we would have come up with on our own. Sometimes our hearts might not be in it. Sometimes the joy just won't be there. Sometimes there will be no fulfillment, no passion. Sometimes it will be lonely. Often, we will be unappreciated or even unnoticed. There may be no immediate gratification or tangible results. Often, we will meet opposition and resistance. And in those times, all we will have to go on is what Buechner calls a "lump in the throat" and "an itching in the feet" —

---

5 Frederick Buechner. *The Alphabet of Grace* (New York: Walker and Company, 1970), 109-110.

that inward, unexplainable assurance that this is who we are and what we have to do. And sometimes that inner compulsion will be all that keeps us going. Sometimes the best reason, the highest reason, the noblest reason for doing the things we do is because we have to.

The organist just learned two hours before coming to church that morning that her son had been arrested for possession of drugs. When she learned of the news, she got ready and went to church. The people in the sanctuary that day said she had never played more beautifully. After the service, one of her closest friends who knew of her son's arrest came up to her and said, "You have never played more beautifully than you did this morning. How could you even make yourself come to church and then play so beautifully when you were so emotionally distressed? She answered, "I came to church and played the organ this morning because I am the organist. It is who I am. It is what I do."

There was a time in my own life many years ago when I agonized over a decision to leave the ministry to which I had been called. For many reasons, I had no passion, no desire, and no energy to continue doing my work. At that time, I was preaching almost every Sunday and felt so hypocritical because I had always been conditioned to believe that, if my heart was not in it (and mine surely was not in it), then I shouldn't be doing it. It seemed so forced to stand up week after week and speak on behalf of God to that congregation when down deep inside I felt so empty.

At first, I didn't quit because I needed a job to support my children. But later, when I had an opportunity to take another kind of job, I couldn't do it. At the time, I never could really understand why I kept on. It didn't seem to make sense to me at the time, but I kept on not because I wanted to, not because I was receiving satisfaction and fulfillment, not because I felt like it, but because I *had* to. And I learned through that agonizing time in my life that there is incredible energy available to those who *have* to do things. I *had* to do what I was doing — to be true to the

God who made me, to the Savior who redeemed me, to the Spirit who prompted me, to the church who supported me, and to myself as well.

Throughout my ministry, I have watched friends and family members go through so many hardships, so many crises, so many losses that they really were not able to endure, saying, "I don't think I can do this another day." Yet somehow, they did make it through another day, and then another — all because they had to. We do what we have to do. And when necessity is laid upon us from God, there is incredible energy and strength available to us. So what is it that you know in your heart you *have* to do?

When I was a young boy, I learned how to pray by listening to the grown-ups in my church. Every Sunday, I listened as the spiritual giants in my home church offered their prayers to God. And as I listened, I heard certain phrases repeated over and over again, and eventually began incorporating those phrases into my own prayers without ever really giving them much thought. "Thank You for the missionaries who go across the sea to tell others about Jesus," one would say. "Thank You for Jesus who died on the cross to save us from our sins," another would say. And then around the time of the offering, you could count on someone to ask God to "bless the gift and the giver." Then there were those other clichés that never seemed to make much sense, but seemed to catch on like, "Bless each and every man, woman, boy, and girl" (and I remember thinking that just about covers everyone) and my personal favorite: "Lead, guide, and direct us" (and I never really understood why it was always necessary to use all three words and always in that order). There were some things you just didn't question. But the phrase that, as a seven-year-old boy, I thought was the most impressive was the one used by my former pastor, Jim Holston, who was always asking God to "forgive us of our sins of omission and commission."

Well, like I said, I learned to pray by listening to these experts, and without even realizing it, I began to incorporate these clichés into my prayers. I didn't know what any of them meant, but I was proud to use them. I will never forget one Sunday evening in what was then called "Training Union," my teachers, Harry and Julia Coleman, asked me to lead in prayer, which I was glad to do. Trying to impress my peers and my teachers, I strung together all of the clichés I could remember, as I prayed, "Dear God, thank You for the missionaries who go across the sea to tell others about Jesus. Bless the gift and the giver. Bless each and every man, woman, boy, and girl. Lead, guide, and direct us. And forgive us of our sins of omission and commission. In Jesus's name, amen." After the prayer, Mrs. Coleman thanked me for my prayer and then asked me to explain sins of omission and commission to the class. And I knew I had gotten caught. I didn't even know enough to make an educated guess. And so Mrs. Coleman used some class time that night to explain the meaning of sins of omission and commission. And for the first time in my life I began to realize that I could sin without ever doing anything, and that the easiest and most grievous sin of all was the sin of knowing what I have to do and failing to do it.

The writer of the letter of James wrote that those who know what is right to do and fail to do it, for them it is sin. Now, of course we can be forgiven for the sin of doing nothing, but often the consequences of our sin, the devastating impact of our sin can be lasting. And the reality is, as the letter of James says in that same passage, we can never recover or duplicate missed opportunities. Life is like a vapor, James wrote, a mist that appears for a short time and then vanishes — here today, and gone tomorrow. Life is slipping "through our fingers like sand."[6] As the great

---

6 Gloria Gaither, *We Have This Moment Today,* Copyright © 1975 Hanna Street Music (BMI) (adm. at CapitolCMGPublishing.com) All rights reserved. Used by permission.

theologian, Yogi Berra, said, "It gets late early."⁷ In fact, it gets real late real early. But the same Yogi Berra said, "It ain't over till it's over."⁸ That is why it is so important to do now what we know in our hearts we have to do.

During the summer each year, the Nominating Committee in our church gets busy asking people to do the many jobs that have to be done in the church. And there are always people in the church who have their excuses, I mean reasons, why they cannot do things they are asked to do. And seriously, many of these reasons are valid. But as I listen to these same explanations year after year, I cannot help but wonder to myself: "Where is the sense of necessity? Are there no people any more who do things because they *have* to do them? Where are the people who will say, 'Count on me. I don't know how, but I'll do what I have to do for this church that I love so much. I may not always like it, it may not always make me feel warm and fuzzy, it may be terribly inconvenient, it may not always bring me joy, but I know in my heart that this is something I *have* to do. This is why God made me, this is what God has called me to do, and this is what I *have* to do' "?

God always has ways of bringing us around. With Paul, it was a blinding light on a Damascus road. But there came a time when Paul knew what he had to do, and he spent the rest of his life doing it. His life was filled with many heartbreaks, disappointments, persecutions, afflictions, crises, and conflicts — enough to make anybody want to quit. But he did what he had to do. And sometimes that is the real test of discipleship. Doing the things that bring us bliss, pleasure, satisfaction, and fulfillment comes naturally. But doing the things we would prefer not to

---

7 Lawrence Peter Berra. *Yogi: It Ain't Over* (New York: McGraw-Hill Publishing Company, 1989), 5-6.
8 Ibid.

do, the things that bring us more pain than pleasure, the things we *have* to do shapes us into the people God would have us be.

Paul said, "An obligation is laid upon me" (1 Corinthians 9:16). An obligation is laid upon us, too. For some of the most important work we will ever do is work that we would not have chosen, but work that God has chosen for us to do. And woe be to us if we do not. Amen.

GET OUT OF THE BOAT

MATTHEW 14:22-33

---

²² *Immediately he made the disciples get into a boat and go on ahead to the other side, while he dismissed the crowds.* ²³ *And after he had dismissed the crowds, he went up the mountain by himself to pray. When evening came, he was there alone,* ²⁴ *but by this time the boat, battered by the waves, was far from the land, for the wind was against them.* ²⁵ *And early in the morning he came walking toward them on the sea.* ²⁶ *But when the disciples saw him walking on the sea, they were terrified, saying, "It is a ghost!" And they cried out in fear.* ²⁷ *But immediately Jesus spoke to them and said, "Take heart, it is I; do not be afraid."*

²⁸ *Peter answered him, "Lord, if it is you, command me to come to you on the water."* ²⁹ *He said, "Come." So Peter got out of the boat, started walking on the water, and came toward Jesus.* ³⁰ *But when he noticed the strong wind, he became frightened, and, beginning to sink, he cried out, "Lord, save me!"* ³¹ *Jesus immediately reached out his hand and caught him, saying to him, "You of little faith, why did you doubt?"* ³² *When they got into the boat, the wind ceased.* ³³ *And those in the boat worshiped him, saying, "Truly you are the Son of God."*

Following Jesus might be one of the most irrational things you will ever do. From time to time, I will hear people make statements like these: "I know God expects us to have faith, but God also expects us to use common sense ... God gave us a mind and expects us to use it ... God does not expect us to be foolish." And those statements are certainly true as far as they go. But in the Bible that I read, God is always calling people to do irrational things that make about as much sense as trying to walk on water.

As Matthew tells the story, Jesus had just fed a crowd of several thousand people by miraculously multiplying five loaves and two fish. And there were, by all counts, twelve baskets of leftovers. Because of my unhealthy appetite, that is not an unimportant detail. I am still wondering what happened to those leftovers and who got to take them home. Anyway, it was after that display of power that Jesus made His disciples get into a boat and precede Him to the other side of the Sea of Galilee to get away from the crowds. In the meantime, possibly misunderstood by the crowds and even by the twelve, Jesus went up into the hills by Himself to pray. While Jesus prayed alone, the disciples found themselves in the middle of the Sea, which was about four and a half miles wide, when a storm began to rock the boat. Sometime between 3:00 a.m. and 6:00 a.m., the darkest time of the night, in the midst of the storm, Jesus came to them walking on the Sea. Understandably, when they saw the form of someone walking toward them on the storm-tossed Sea, they were terrified and frantic. All of a sudden, they started believing in ghosts because there was no rational explanation for what they were seeing. But some things that are not rational are real. In fact, contrary to what we have been conditioned to believe, the things that are most real are the things which cannot be explained on the basis of reason. About the time the disciples' fear reached a feverish pitch, Jesus spoke to them: "Take heart, I am, have no fear." Now isn't that about the most irrational statement you have ever heard? What is reasonable about that? "Jesus," the disciples must have thought, "Have you lost your mind? We are in the middle of a lake, and in case you haven't noticed, there is a storm going on, and somebody is walking toward us on the water. And now, our twelve baskets of leftovers have gotten soggy. And you want us to calm down? I'm sorry, someone has to use some common sense here. Somebody has to introduce some sanity into this discussion." But it is at this point in the story that we learn something very important about following Jesus. Jesus said, "Because I am, you have nothing to fear, no reason to be afraid. I may be all you have, but I am all you need."

Something compelled Peter at that moment to speak up. "Lord, can I do that? Can I try?" Pleased and maybe even amused by Peter's request, Jesus said, "Sure. Come on." And without thinking, Peter got out of the boat and began walking on the water. How do I know that Peter didn't think about it? Because if he had thought about it, he never would have gotten out of the boat. I mean God does expect us to use common sense, right?

As He did with Peter that night, Jesus is always calling us to follow Him, leave the security and comfort of the boat, and maybe even do something irrational or risky for the sheer pleasure of being with Jesus. About the time Peter reached Jesus on the water, he must have realized how foolish and irrational his behavior was. Matthew says that when Peter saw how windy it was, he started panicking, and then began to sink. And if he didn't realize how irrational his behavior was before he started to sink, the thought surely crossed his mind while he was sinking. "You know this really was pretty crazy of me to think that I could do what Jesus was doing. This was not a very smart idea," Peter must have thought when he realized that he was no longer on top of things (so to speak). It was right about then that Peter cried out. "ᴛ save me!" And Jesus did. He reached out His hand and puᵗ
the boat. "You of little faith, why did you doubt?" Jesus ?

was one question for which even Peter did not have an answer. About the time Peter and Jesus got into the boat, the wind ceased, and the disciples used that experience and that moment of calm as an occasion to worship Jesus saying, "Truly You are the Son of God."

Usually when I hear people reflect on this passage, the focus is on the reason Peter began to sink. "He took his eyes off Jesus," we've always been told. But the text never says that. What intrigues me about this text is not what caused Peter to sink, but what caused Peter to get out of the boat in the first place. Remember, there were presumably twelve disciples in the boat, but only one got out of the boat. What caused Peter to get out of the boat, and the other disciples to stay in it? What was so different about Peter? For a moment, let's forget about why Peter began to sink long enough to remember that at least he got out of the boat, which is more than you can say for the rest of the disciples, and more than you can say about most of us.

One of the best ways to understand and apply the Bible is to find yourself in it. And when I read this story, there is no question where I am in it. I am one of the those who had the good sense to stay in the boat — not only because I can't swim (although that's a big part of it), but also because I pride myself in being a very rational person. And while I'm confessing, I may as well admit that not only am I in the boat, but I am probably ridiculing Peter for venturing out: "Peter, God expects you to use a little common sense." You see, it is easy enough to ridicule Peter for his irrational behavior while we stay in the safety of the boat. When Peter began to sink, I wouldn't be able to resist saying to Peter, "I knew that was a stupid idea. Your irrational behavior was a recipe for failure. I hope you will outgrow this immature, idealistic phase you are going through. Now get back in, and don't rock the boat anymore."

On the floor of the United States Senate in January of 1949, Chaplain Peter Marshall prayed, "Help us to see that it is better to fail in a cause that will ultimately succeed than to succeed in a cause that will ultimately fail." Sure, there was a point at which Peter began to sink — but at least he was with Jesus, doing what Jesus was doing. At least He was close enough to Jesus for Jesus to take his hand and keep him from sinking. It is always better to fail with Jesus than to succeed apart from Him. It is always better to be where Jesus is in danger than to be apart from Jesus in safety. Matthew does not mean to teach that failure does not matter, but that Jesus does not fail even when we do. And if Jesus could say that Peter had little faith, what does that say about the faith of the disciples who stayed in the security of the boat? And what does that say about our faith? You see, it was not so much how much faith Peter had. It was what he did with it.

What was different about Peter? What could possibly motivate a person to get out of the boat and do such an irrational thing? The text does not say, but it does imply that Peter just wanted to be where Jesus was and do what Jesus was doing. Peter must have had a desire to join Jesus, a desire so passionate and consuming that he would leave the comfort and security of the boat just for the sheer joy of being with Jesus.

In the life of faith, it is easy for us to become so falsely secure and comfortable that we lose the will to get out of the boat. Rather than being driven by a passionate desire to join Jesus, it is so easy for us to be driven instead by a desire to do the rational thing, to do the safe thing, to keep the familiar system in place in which we have a vested interest, and to preserve the status quo that makes us feel safe. There might have been a time in our discipleship when we would have jumped at the chance to be where Jesus was. But not anymore. And those who do seem to be driven by an irrational desire to follow Jesus are often marginalized, if not openly ridiculed for being fanatical. But if we are going to be where Jesus is, we are going to have to get out of the boat, engage in holy experiments, and risk failure, trusting that even if we begin to sink, Jesus will reach out His hand and lift us up. The mission of the church, and the individuals in it, is to be where Jesus is and do what Jesus does. That will always seem irrational to some people — even in the church.

So, what is it that is keeping you from joining Jesus? To be where Jesus is doing what Jesus does, you will have to get out of the boat. For some of us, that may mean that we need to give up financial security. "… Sell your possessions and give the money to the poor …," Jesus once said to a young man (Matthew 19:21). That sounds pretty irrational to me. For some of us, that may mean that we will need to make following Jesus an even higher priority than family concerns: "Let the dead bury their own dead," Jesus said to one man who wanted to bury his father before following Jesus (Matthew 8:22), and to another, He said, "Whoever loves father or mother more than me is not worthy of me" (Matthew 10:37). Give up everything to follow Jesus? Leave your family behind?

Come to think of it, Peter was called upon to do both the first time Jesus called him to get out of the boat. You see, this was not the first time Peter got out of a boat to be with Jesus. Remember the story? Peter left his fishing net, which was his means of financial security, and his family behind to follow Jesus. There was nothing rational about Peter's decision to follow Jesus. But if you want to be where Jesus is and do what Jesus does, you have to get out of the boat. And only you will know what that means for you. What is holding you back from getting out of the boat? Do you find the security of the boat more appealing than the joy of being with Jesus?

One could argue that it was a lot easier for Peter to find Jesus than it is for us. I mean there He was, plain as day, walking on the water. But if we are going to find Jesus today, how and where would we find

Him? Near the end of Matthew's Gospel, Jesus gives us some clues about where and how to find Him. We will have to be willing to leave our comfort zones and give up some of our security. We will have to be willing to get out of the boat, so to speak. Jesus said that if we are going to be where He is, we may have to leave the familiarity of where we are and find the hungry, the thirsty, the naked, the prisoner, the stranger, and the sick — because when we find them, we will find Him. We may have to take some risks like Peter did. It may be irrational. But there is nothing to compare with the joy of being with Jesus, doing what He is doing, and trusting that, even when we fail, we will be close enough to Him, and He will be close enough to us, to take us by the hand and lift us up.

How to Understand the Bible
LUKE 24:36-48

⁳⁶ While they were talking about this, Jesus himself stood among them and said to them, "Peace be with you." ⁳⁷ They were startled and terrified, and thought that they were seeing a ghost. ⁳⁸ He said to them, "Why are you frightened, and why do doubts arise in your hearts? ⁳⁹ Look at my hands and my feet; see that it is I myself. Touch me and see; for a ghost does not have flesh and bones as you see that I have." ⁴⁰ And when he had said this, he showed them his hands and his feet. ⁴¹ While in their joy they were disbelieving and still wondering, he said to them, "Have you anything here to eat?" ⁴² They gave him a piece of broiled fish, ⁴³ and he took it and ate in their presence.

⁴⁴ Then he said to them, "These are my words that I spoke to you while I was still with you — that everything written about me in the law of Moses, the prophets, and the psalms must be fulfilled." ⁴⁵ Then he opened their minds to understand the scriptures, ⁴⁶ and he said to them, "Thus it is written, that the Messiah is to suffer and to rise from the dead on the third day, ⁴⁷ and that repentance and forgiveness of sins is to be proclaimed in his name to all nations, beginning from Jerusalem. ⁴⁸ You are witnesses of these things.

In my kind of work, I constantly hear people say that the Bible doesn't make sense to them. And, to be honest, it is not the easiest book to interpret. Some of that is because it is not just one book. It is actually a collection of books written by many authors over a period of centuries. The books are not all in chronological order. Some books report the same history almost verbatim, while others interpret the same history in different ways. So it is not uncommon for me to hear people say that they started reading the Bible, but finally got lost and gave up.

In modern times, there are all kinds of Bible study resources that are designed to help us make sense of the Bible. These days, there are so-called "Bibles for Dummies" and all kinds of daily Bible reading plans. There are study Bibles that have notes in the margins or at the bottom that are there to explain each passage. There are Bible apps and on-line resources that provide explanation and context, and even help with the Hebrew and Greek languages if you want to get that deep into it. There are countless translations and paraphrases of the Scripture that make the ancient text come alive in contemporary language. There are topical Bibles and chronological Bibles. In fact, there are so many resources out there that many of us do not even know where to start, or which ones to trust. So how do you understand the Bible?

Well, for followers of Jesus, the surest way to understand the Scripture is to let Jesus explain it to us, which is what He did for His disciples in the story we just read. Luke says the risen Christ "opened their minds to understand the Scriptures" (Luke 24:45). And therein was one the biggest challenges Jesus ever faced: opening the minds of His disciples. It is one of the biggest challenges any teacher of Scripture faces. How do you get people to approach the Scripture with an open mind when they presume they already know what it says, what it *should* say, or what it means? How do you get people to open their minds without making them so gullible that they will fall for anything? How can we open our minds *enough* without opening them *so much* that the Scripture can mean whatever they want it to mean?

At the time Luke's Gospel was written, of course, there was no New Testament. So, the only Scripture Jesus had was what we call the Old Testament, and He did not even have *all* of the Old Testament. There was "the Law," the Torah, which consisted of the first five books of our Bible: Genesis, Exodus, Leviticus, Numbers, and Deuteronomy — and the Prophets, which consisted of the "Former Prophets" (Joshua, Judges, Samuel, and Kings) and the "Latter Prophets" (Isaiah, Jeremiah, Ezekiel, and the Book of the Twelve, which we call "the minor prophets," the final twelve books in our Old Testament). But by the time Luke's Gospel was written, a third category known as "The Writings" was in the process of being collected and accepted as authoritative Scripture, including the book of Psalms, and gradually including all the other books in our Old Testament. So when Jesus referred to "the Law of Moses, the Prophets, and the Psalms," that was His way of referring to the Bible of His time.

This passage is Luke's description of Jesus's third resurrection appearance. There had been the resurrection appearance to Cleopas and an unidentified disciple on the way to, and at the meal in, Emmaus (Luke 24:13-29a, 29b-32). There had also been an off-stage resurrection appearance to Simon (Luke 24:33-34). And here, the risen Jesus appears for a third time, this time suddenly in the midst of His disciples, offering them peace and demonstrating that He was not some sort of ghost, but had a physical resurrected body (Luke 24:36-42). He ate some broiled fish with them, and then He reminded them of what He had told them before His crucifixion — that everything written about Him in the Law, the Prophets, and the Psalms had to be fulfilled. Of course, that statement required further explanation. So that is when Luke tells us that Jesus opened their minds to understand the Scriptures. In other words, He explained the Bible to His disciples.

Wouldn't you have liked to have been there to hear Jesus explain the Bible? Once He opened the minds of His disciples, He called attention to what He had previously predicted about His own suffering and resurrection. Then He reminded them that the message of repentance and forgiveness should be preached, with the disciples providing eye-witness testimony. And finally, He promised the disciples that they would not have to preach and bear witness in their own power, but would receive power from God to keep the gospel story alive.

Of course, this was not the first time in Luke's Gospel that Jesus had spoken about His impending death and resurrection in terms of divine necessity. What is different about this time is that He was speaking these words *after* His death and resurrection. On the *other* side of Easter, the disciples were able to understand what they could not have imagined *before* Easter. Only now, as the crucified and resurrected Jesus stood among them, inviting them to see His hands and feet with their own eyes and touch Him with their own hands, would they be capable of comprehending how Jesus had fulfilled the prophecies concerning Him.

Luke's approach, unlike Matthew's approach, was not to establish proof texts to show which particular scriptural passages had been fulfilled, but to demonstrate an even larger point — and that is that all Scripture finds its ultimate meaning in the life, death, and resurrection of Jesus.

So how does a Christian understand the Bible? How do followers of Jesus interpret the Scripture? The answer is as simple and profound as this: We interpret all Scripture in the light of who Jesus was, what Jesus said, and what Jesus did. And since the historical Jesus is no longer present with us in the flesh, we understand the Bible as we are guided by the Spirit of Jesus.

Now of course, that sounds good in theory. But how does that actually work? What does it mean to say that we are counting on Jesus to help us understand the Bible? Well, this is where I am indebted to Chuck Poole, who clarified how we can let Jesus explain the Bible to us in our own time. First, we begin with our faith that Jesus gives us our best look at God. And the surest way to get to know Jesus is to read the four Gospels over and over until we get a clear sense of who Jesus is, until we are saturated with the Spirit of the living Christ. Jesus said the Spirit will guide us into all truth. Then when we read the Bible, we filter it through our understanding of Jesus, as we are guided by His Spirit.[9]

Let me give you some examples of how this might work. Let's start with an easy example. Leviticus 24:19-20:

> *When a man causes a disfigurement in his neighbor, as he has done, it shall be done to him, fracture for fracture, eye for eye, tooth for tooth; as he has disfigured a man, he shall be disfigured.*

How does Jesus help us understand this passage? Well, in the Sermon on the Mount, Jesus spoke directly to this issue:

> *You have heard that it was said, "An eye for an eye and a tooth for tooth." But I say to you, "Do not resist one who is evil. But if anyone strikes you on the right cheek, turn to him the other also; and if anyone would sue you and take your coat, let him have your cloak as well ...*

So, in this case, it is clear how Jesus helps us understand the Bible. When someone does something to hurt us, we should not retaliate. We interpret the Old Testament in the light of the New Testament, specifically, the teachings of Jesus.

But what about a more difficult example? Let's say we are trying to

---

9 Charles E. Poole. *Beyond the Broken Lights* (Macon, Georgia: Smyth and Helwys Publishing, Inc., 2000), 89-95.

understand the passage of Scripture in Deuteronomy 21 that says God would approve the stoning of a stubborn child. First of all, if that Scripture had been enforced, neither one of my brothers would be alive today.

> ³² While the Israelites were in the wilderness, a man was found gathering wood on the Sabbath day. ³³ Those who found him gathering wood brought him to Moses and Aaron and the whole assembly, ³⁴ and they kept him in custody, because it was not clear what should be done to him. ³⁵ Then the Lord said to Moses, "The man must die. The whole assembly must stone him outside the camp." ³⁶ So the assembly took him outside the camp and stoned him to death, as the Lord commanded Moses.

Or take the passage in Numbers 15 that says that we should impose the death penalty on someone for picking up sticks on the Sabbath Day. It's in your Bible, too.

> ³² When the Israelites were in the wilderness, they found a man gathering sticks on the sabbath day. ³³ Those who found him gathering sticks brought him to Moses, Aaron, and to the whole congregation. ³⁴ They put him in custody, because it was not clear what should be done to him. ³⁵ Then the Lord said to Moses, "The man shall be put to death; all the congregation shall stone him outside the camp."

If we have read the four Gospels over and over, we might remember the occasion recorded in John's Gospel when an adulteress was about to be stoned, and Jesus intervened, telling the potential stoners that the person there without sin could cast the first stone. One by one, the potential stoners walked away, and the only One who was without sin (Jesus Himself) refused to condemn her.

If the life of Jesus has given us our best look at the way God means for life to be lived, and if the four Gospels have given us our best look at Jesus, then the four Gospels must inform us as we seek to understand Scripture. As Chuck Poole wrote, this approach to Biblical understanding does not place the four Gospels at the top of the Bible and everything else beneath them. Rather, this approach places the four Gospels at the center of the Bible, and everything else around them. This is what is often referred to as the "Christocentric" approach to Scripture: Christ is at the center, and everything else is to be understood by the Spirit of Christ, who is to be the criterion by which all Scripture is to be understood and interpreted. This idea does not mean that we should "Christianize" the Hebrew Scriptures and try to find Jesus on every page of the Old Testament. What it means is that, when we read a passage that seems to bless revenge or advocate slavery or dehumanize women, or whatever, we should always ask ourselves if that is true to the Spirit of Christ.[10] Based on what we know of Jesus through Scripture, what did Jesus *say* about that? What did Jesus *do* about that? What did He teach *us* to do? What were the themes of His ministry? What was His tone in dealing with people? What does He have to teach us about what the Bible really means and how He has fulfilled the Scriptures?

Now if you are tracking with me, then you realize that to understand Scripture in the light of the Spirit of Christ is to venture out on a slippery slope. But the truth is that we are already on a slippery slope any time we try to understand the Bible. And if I am going to be on a slippery slope anyway, I would rather be on it with Jesus, who was the clearest picture of God we will ever see. If understanding the Bible by the

---

10 Ibid.

Spirit of Jesus feels like a slippery slope to us, then we can be sure that Jesus is the One who put us on that slippery slope. He is the One who told us that the Spirit would teach us what we need to know and would remind us of all that Jesus said to us. Jesus said the Spirit would guide us into all truth. And with those words, Jesus put us on the slippery slope of understanding the Bible by the inner nudges and quiet tugs of the Holy Spirit, who will remind us of what Jesus revealed about God.[11]

It can feel perilous, and it can be mysterious. It is not as neat and easy as some people make it out to be. But it is the best and surest way I know to understand the Bible. Let the risen Jesus open our minds and explain it to us, which is what He did for His first disciples and what he continues to do by His Spirit for all of us who will submit to His authority.

---

11 Ibid.

It's Not About You

EPHESIANS 3:14-21

---

[14] For this reason I bow my knees before the Father, [15] from whom every family in heaven and on earth takes its name. [16] I pray that, according to the riches of his glory, he may grant that you may be strengthened in your inner being with power through his Spirit, [17] and that Christ may dwell in your hearts through faith, as you are being rooted and grounded in love. [18] I pray that you may have the power to comprehend, with all the saints, what is the breadth and length and height and depth, [19] and to know the love of Christ that surpasses knowledge, so that you may be filled with all the fullness of God.

[20] Now to him who by the power at work within us is able to accomplish abundantly far more than all we can ask or imagine, [21] to him be glory in the church and in Christ Jesus to all generations, forever and ever. Amen.

Have you ever tried to have a conversation with people about a certain subject, but before the conversation was over, it ended up being about them? It didn't really matter what you started out talking about. Before it was over, the conversation somehow became focused on them. Sometimes psychologists identify this tendency as narcissism, which is defined as a disorder in which a person has an inflated sense of self-importance. Most of us would not be surprised to learn that narcissism is found more commonly in men. Sometimes the cause is genetic and sometimes there are environmental factors. Symptoms include an excessive need for admiration, disregard for others' feelings, an inability to handle any criticism, and a sense of entitlement.

And the most insidious, even paradoxical, quality of narcissists is that, for all of their self-centeredness, they are not self-aware.

As I begin this sermon, it is only fair to issue a warning: "Caution: The sermon you are about to hear has very little to do with you. If you came here hoping that the sermon will help you live a happy, fulfilled, stress-free life, this sermon will be a tremendous disappointment to you. If you need help in raising your children, managing your money, or making a good impression at work, this sermon will frustrate you more than it will help you."

The pastor in the very first church I served influenced me in so many ways. He was different — downright weird, in fact. Of course, that word could be used to describe all the pastors with whom I have worked. I think you have to be weird to *be* a pastor. And if you are not weird *before* you become a pastor, you will *become* weird if you stay one any length of time. Bill Marler made a sure and certain impression on me. He had some very definite ideas about worship and preaching, and some of his views did not go over big in the churches he served. But they made a lasting impression on me. And though I was always sure that he was weird, I was also pretty sure he was right.

Well, one Sunday, after the worship service, one of the more outspoken women in the church came up to him and said, "Bill, nothing personal, but I just don't get anything out of your preaching. I have a hard time applying your sermons to my life. I want help in living my life, but your sermons almost never give me the help I need." I was standing right there when she said it, and I couldn't believe what I was hearing. If she had said that to me, I would have been crushed and devastated. I would have apologized profusely and would have promised to do better. But here is what he said. "Where did you get the idea that every sermon is supposed to be about you? Who told you that you are always supposed to *get* something out of a sermon? You weren't *born* with that idea in that head. So, from where did that idea come? And why do you think that every passage of Scripture is supposed to be about you?" She was shocked. And she was speechless. And believe me, it was not easy to make that woman speechless. But she never said anything else about his preaching.

Shortly after that exchange, he retired. So, I am not recommending Bill's approach to pastoral ministry unless a pastor is about to retire, but I *am* suggesting that Bill's questions are worth considering because I hear those kinds of statements all the time. Where *did* we get the idea that every sermon is supposed to be applied to our lives? Who told us that we are always supposed to *get* something out of a sermon? And what makes us think that the Bible is primarily about us anyway? Isn't that a pretty narcissistic view of the Bible?

In every church I have ever served, there have been people who have left the church claiming that they were not being fed, although most of them looked pretty well fed to me. Some have claimed that the worship was not appealing to them. Others complained that the service was boring. But underlying all of these complaints is the consumer-based assumption that we come to church to have our needs met. And if this church doesn't meet my needs, I will go to a church that does because church is all about me — what meets *my* needs, what appeals to *my* interests, what makes me feel good, and what entertains *me*.

In one of his loftiest and most sublime letters, with majestic language, Paul goes to great lengths to describe how the glory of *God* spills over into the glory of *Christ*, whose glory overflows into the *church*, so that the glory of the church drenches the whole *universe*.[12]

It is amazing that Paul can see all of that from a prison cell, as plain as day. But he can. In spite of his circumstances, he receives and then gives a grand and glorious vision of God.

Ephesians is like so many other letters of Paul. Before the letter takes on a practical tone, before Paul ever gets around to describing who *we* are, he presents a captivating and compelling vision of who *God* is. Before Paul gets to the practical application in chapters four through six, in which he describes what *we* are to do and how *we* are to act, he spends the first half of the letter describing what *God* does and how *God* acts. We are not ready to learn about our*selves* until we have first learned about *God*. First things first. As early as chapter 1, Paul makes the stunning claim that our purpose in life is not to be pleased, but to learn what pleases God. Our purpose, according to Paul, is not to *get*, but to *give*; not to be *filled* but to be *emptied*; not to *consume*, but to *be consumed*. We were destined and appointed to live not for our own fulfillment, but, in the words of Paul, "for the praise of God's glory."

And yet this idea flies in the face of everything we have been conditioned to believe as good Americans. Democratic capitalism, which, I believe, is the best economic system, for all its advantages, feeds off the assumption that people will act in their own best interests. From the earliest age, we are conditioned by our culture to be good consumers and to pursue our own happiness. And we bring all those instincts to church with us. The church, in turn, often is guilty of feeding our self-centeredness by giving us what we want and what the market demands. In order to survive, many churches have to design their programs and ministries with a competitive mindset. If we don't offer

---

[12] Barbara Brown Taylor. *Home by Another Way* (Boston: Cowley Publications, 1999), 137.

what the church down the street offers, we will lose people. If we don't give people what they want, they'll take their business somewhere else. And so people bounce around from church to church, shopping for a church like they would shop for any other product or service — trying to get the most they can for the least investment. So often, the church is guilty of taking basically selfish, self-absorbed people, and making them even more selfish by catering to their whims.

So it comes as no surprise, then, that people who have been thoroughly immersed in a consumer-oriented culture, bring those attitudes with them to church. "If the Bible has nothing to do with me, then it must be of no value. If your sermon cannot reduce the mystery of the Bible to a series of suggestions about how I can live a happy, productive life, then why should I be interested in it? If I am bored by church, if I do not get anything out of it, if I am not entertained by it, then it must be of no value — because it's all about me. Therefore, I will skip the parts of the Bible that are boring and get to the good stuff, you know, the stuff about *me*, the stuff that will help *me*, the stuff that will make *my* life easier and happier."

It is essentially the same argument many children make about some of the subjects they have to take in school, which are the same arguments I made when I was in school. Why should I have to take a course in chemistry if I am never going to use that information? Why should I study geometry if it won't help me get a job? If I can't use it, then why bother with it? But now that I am as old as I am, I cannot explain how, but I know that my life is richer and fuller because I studied some of those "useless subjects." Somehow, I learned a little more about the immensity and complexity of the world in which I live. If nothing else, I learned how much I don't know — and just knowing how much I don't know has made me a little more aware of what I do know. And if that is true of the world of physics and chemistry and geometry, how much more true is it of the glory of God?

And so a whole culture of religious celebrities have figured out how to cash in on the demands of the market. I did a search this week of some of the best sellers in Christian bookstores and was amazed at the number of books that begin with the words, "How to ..." *How to Be a Praying Mom, How to Live by Faith in an Uncertain World, How to Talk about Jesus without Freaking Out, How to Pursue Purity in a Sex-Saturated World, How to Recognize Bad Reasoning, How to Make Choices You Won't Regret, How to Manage Your Money, How to Understand Your Past to Ensure a Healthier Future, How to Fight for Joy, How to Hear from God, How to Respond When You Feel Mistreated, How to Talk to Your Child About Sex.* The preachers who draw the crowds and write the books are the ones who have reduced the mysteries of God to a simple, user-friendly outline: *Seven Ways to Have a Healthy Marriage, Four Easy Steps to a Worry-Free Life, Twelve Paths to Financial Security, Six Rules for Successful Living.* But some of us read the Bible and don't find it to be a "how-to" kind of book.

And so it may come as a shock for some of us to discover that, sometimes, it is not about us. The Bible is not primarily about us. It is primarily about God. Life is not primarily about *getting* something *from* God. It is primarily about *giving* something *to* God. And worship is the one activity that gets us out of our self-absorbed world long enough to remind us that there is a power more grand and more glorious than anything we could ever ask or think. You may not recognize the value of it, but it does you more good than you may realize to leave your loud, busy, self-indulgent lifestyle and enter the quietness and beauty of a place of worship. It may seem routine to you, but it is good for you to stand and sing, "Praise God, from whom all blessings flow. Praise Him, all creatures here below. Praise Him above, ye heavenly hosts, praise Father, Son, and Holy Ghost."[13] This worship may

---

13 Thomas Ken. *Praise God, from Whom All Blessings Flow.* Public domain.

be the one hour a week when we do not focus on what appeals to us, but rather on what appeals to God. And if we are bored by what happens here, that may say more about us than it does about the worship leaders.

Paul wrote, "I bow my knees" (i.e., "I assume a posture of worship and humility") "before the Father, by whom every family in heaven and on earth is named (Ephesians 3:14-15). The act of kneeling is a symbolic way of demonstrating that we are not in a position to make demands upon God, but instead, we are in a position to submit to the will of God. Just as Jesus knelt in the Garden of Gethsemane to submit to the will of God, so Paul, by kneeling, recognized that we are caught up in the eternal plan of God, that the strength given to us through the Spirit, the presence of the living Christ made known to us through faith and grounded in love, all of the riches of God's glory are showered upon us as we know Christ.

In Philippians, Paul wrote that for him to live is Christ, to know Him and the power of His resurrection, to live for the praise of His glory. And what is most striking to me is that Paul prayed for the Ephesians — not that they might be happy, not that they might learn how to live productive lives, not that they might be famous or wealthy, but that they might "comprehend, with all the saints, what is the breadth and length and height and depth, and to know the love of Christ that surpasses knowledge, so that they may be filled with all the fullness of God" (Ephesians 3:18-19). And then Paul went on to conclude this section of Ephesians with these words: "Now to him who by the power at work within us is able to accomplish abundantly far more than all we can ask or imagine, to him be glory in the church and in Christ Jesus to all generations, forever and ever. Amen" (Ephesians 3:20-21). And only then, is Paul ready to say in the first verse of chapter 4, "Therefore … I beg you to lead a life that is worthy of the One who has called you …"

Now that you have caught a glimpse of who God is — the Father, the Son, and the Spirit — and how the church fits into God's eternal plan, now we are ready to talk about how your life is caught up in the fullness of God. The psalmist prayed, "In your light we see light" (Psalm 36:9). There comes a time when we must learn how to live our lives, but only after we have considered the breadth, the length, the height, and the depth of the love of Christ. I am not very familiar with contemporary Christian music, but there is a song that says, "I'm coming back to the heart of worship, and it's all about You, it's all about You, Jesus."[14]

In our tradition, we gather for worship in a sanctuary, away from the noises and distractions of the world. We hear the majestic sounds of the pipe organ. We stand to sing the hymns of praise that remind us that God is worthy of worship. We hear the choir's voices blending together in beautiful harmony. We hear the Scripture read from the ancient book and preached. We sing a final song, have a closing prayer or benediction, and then we leave. One might ask, "What good did any of that do? My life is still in the same mess it was in before I ever came here. I got nothing specific to help me face the challenges of my life. The world still suffers. Was this hour a total waste of time, a fantasy trip, an escape? Or is worship its own reward? There are some things in life that are worth doing just for the sake of doing them. And we are richer for doing them. I don't know about you, but I need to be reminded that it's not always, or even primarily, about me.

---

14 Matt Redman. *The Heart of Worship*. Copyright © 1999 Thankyou Music (PRS) (adm. worldwide at CapitolCMGPublishing.com excluding the UK & Europe which is adm. at IntegratedRights.com) All rights reserved. Used by permission.

LIFE IS HARD, BUT GOD IS FAITHFUL
1 CORINTHIANS 10:1-13

¹ I do not want you to be unaware, brothers and sisters, that our ancestors were all under the cloud, and all passed through the sea, ² and all were baptized into Moses in the cloud and in the sea, ³ and all ate the same spiritual food, ⁴ and all drank the same spiritual drink. For they drank from the spiritual rock that followed them, and the rock was Christ. ⁵ Nevertheless, God was not pleased with most of them, and they were struck down in the wilderness.

⁶ Now these things occurred as examples for us, so that we might not desire evil as they did. ⁷ Do not become idolaters as some of them did; as it is written, "The people sat down to eat and drink, and they rose up to play." ⁸ We must not indulge in sexual immorality as some of them did, and twenty-three thousand fell in a single day. ⁹ We must not put Christ to the test, as some of them did, and were destroyed by serpents. ¹⁰ And do not complain as some of them did, and were destroyed by the destroyer. ¹¹ These things happened to them to serve as an example, and they were written down to instruct us, on whom the ends of the ages have come. ¹² So if you think you are standing, watch out that you do not fall. ¹³ No testing has overtaken you that is not common to everyone. God is faithful, and he will not let you be tested beyond your strength, but with the testing he will also provide the way out so that you may be able to endure it.

When I was in seminary, my preaching professor advised us to do something that seemed a little strange to me at the time. He said that sometime early in the week, while we were still thinking about how to develop the sermon for the coming Sunday, we needed to walk into the empty sanctuary, stand behind the pulpit, look at the empty pews, and picture who would probably be sitting in those pews this Sunday. He said that, if we are the kind of pastors we should be, we should know the people to whom we were preaching. We should know what they are going through. We should try to imagine who might be present, where they might be sitting, how they will hear the sermon, how they might filter our sermons through their own experiences. We should picture the people sitting in the pews and ask ourselves: "What are their joys? What are their sorrows? What are their needs? What are their relationships like? What will be on their minds when they come into the sanctuary and take their seats this Sunday? What private pain will they be hiding?" And of course, the best way to know the answers to those questions is to get to know the people to whom you preach and share your life with them.

Well, when you get desperate enough as a preacher, you will even resort to taking your professor's advice. Desperate times call for desperate measures, and I was pretty desperate when I was preparing this sermon. I was getting nowhere fast. Nothing was coming to me. I had read the passage and all the commentaries I could find. I had read sermons by other preachers on this passage, but I was still stuck. So, I waited until no one else was around (because the staff here already thinks I'm weird enough), and I walked into the sanctuary with my Bible open to this passage of Scripture from First Corinthians. I tried to picture who might be here today, where you might be sitting, what you might be going through, and what you might need to hear from God today. Of course, I don't know everything there is to know about you. Some of you I do not know at all. But, as I started picturing your faces in my mind's eye and started thinking about the particular challenges some of you are facing, I started realizing that there is a common thread that is woven throughout the fabric of all of our experiences. Though the particular details of your situations are unique to you, and the way you respond to your situation varies from person to person, we all know what it is like to have the claims of our faith tested by the harsh realities of life. **Life is hard.**

And when we are going through those hard times, we tend to feel like we are all alone. It is so easy to sing the blues: "Nobody knows the trouble I've seen." We look around and we see everybody else here at church. They all seem to have their lives together. Just look around. You dress up well. Your life seems to be under control. Look around and you might get the impression that no one else here would understand what you are going through. Well, look again. If there is one thing I have learned by doing this kind of work, it is this. No one is as together as he or she may seem. And the ones who seem to be the most secure are often the most vulnerable. Paul wrote to the Corinthians, "No testing has overtaken you that is not common to everyone" (1 Corinthians 10:13). I realize that the translation you may be using may use the word *temptation* instead of *testing*. It is a form of the same word used by Paul in verse 9, when he writes, "We must not put the Lord to the test." So, the same word translated "test" in verse 9 is often translated "temptation," as in verse 13. The reason is that the Greek word Paul used can carry with it both shades of meaning. It can mean temptation in the sense of being misled into sin. Or it can mean a trial or testing, having one's faith put to the test. It can refer to the everyday testings of life, or it can refer to the ultimate trial or testing which would cause us to deny or fall away from our faith and trust in God. In other words, that single word pretty much covers any kind of test, temptation, or trial that would challenge and threaten the claims and strength of our faith.

One of the particular testings that the Corinthians were facing was addressed by Paul in chapter 8 and is re-addressed in verse 14 of chapter 10. It is a test which, in many ways, seems far-removed from our experience. There in that cosmopolitan, seaport city, there were many religious people who offered sacrifices to pagan gods. The meat from those sacrifices was then sold to anyone who would buy it. Some Christians in Corinth, as a matter of principle, were opposed to buying and eating meat that had been sacrificed to idols in worship. "It's just not right," they thought. "We need to make a clean break between ourselves and the pagans. We need to avoid even the appearance of participating in idolatry." Other Christians didn't have a problem with it. They figured, "You can't totally separate yourself from the culture around you. You've got to learn to live in the world without being contaminated by it. Meat is meat. It doesn't matter if it has been sacrificed to a pagan god or not, because such gods do not really exist anyway. And besides, we are free and secure in Christ." It was a test for the Corinthians, and it was a potentially divisive issue for the church. So, Paul was writing to give guidance as they faced this challenge. **Life is hard.**

Being a student of the Hebrew Scriptures, Paul realized the danger of false security, religious smugness, and spiritual superiority. "Remember how God led the covenant people out of Egyptian slavery, opening the Red Sea that they might pass through it on dry land? Do you remember how God led them by a cloud toward the land of promise, giving them manna from heaven and water in the desert?" For Paul, passing through the Red Sea gave the Old Testament people the same sense of false security that baptism gave to the New Testament people. Likewise, eating the manna and drinking the water gave the old covenant people the same kind of false security as partaking of the Lord's Supper gave the new covenant people. Like the people of Israel, the Corinthians felt overconfident not in God, but in their privileged status. They were God's chosen people, and they began to develop an over-inflated sense of self-sufficiency. But God was neither pleased nor impressed. Although God satisfied their needs, they did not satisfy God's requirements. Somehow, they began to feel like they deserved their privileged status and that nothing could cause them to fall. But the presence of divine providence does not mean the absence of divine judgment. As the writer of Proverbs put it, "Pride goes before destruction, and a haughty spirit before a fall" (Proverbs 16:18). Paul said it this way, "So if you think you are standing, watch out that you do not fall" (1 Corinthians 10:12). **Life is hard.**

Like the people of Israel in the wilderness, the Corinthians were flirting with idolatry and were being seduced by its charms. "We must not put the Lord to the test," Paul wrote. "We must not accept God's gracious provision and then presume upon it. We should learn from their mistakes," Paul warned. "These things happened to them as a warning, but they were written down for *our* instruction" (my paraphrase of 1 Corinthians 10:9-11). We ignore their experiences to our own peril. Despite all of God's provisions for them, the people of Israel grew impatient with God and began worshiping a golden calf. Later in the wilderness, they were seduced by the Moabites and their religion, and began to make sacrifices to their gods — and as a result, God's judgment fell upon some 23,000 of them who died by a plague in a single day. On another occasion, the people of Israel became impatient as they made their way around the land of Edom. They put the Lord to the test by complaining that they had no food and were destroyed by serpents. Time after time, they presumed upon God's goodness, took advantage of God's provisions, and began to rely on their own resourcefulness. And there were disastrous consequences. They faced the tests and failed them, and they had no one to blame but themselves. **Life is hard.**

They tried to blame God, but the charge just wouldn't stick. God had led them out of slavery and opened the waters of the Red Sea for them to pass through on dry land. God led them toward the land of promise with a cloud by day and a pillar of fire by night. God fed them with bread from heaven and gave them water to drink from a rock. **Life is hard ... but God is faithful.** God always is faithful.

Our problem is never God's lack of faithfulness. It is ours. The covenant between God and God's people is not a contract between equal parties. God is always making a way to keep promises even when we do not keep ours.

Sometimes God's faithfulness is shown in what God *prevents*. God "will not let you be tested beyond your strength," Paul wrote (1 Corinthians 10:13). And so whatever kind of testing you may be facing, it is not more than you can bear. I cannot tell you how many times I have heard people say and have said myself, "I do not think I can live with this pain another day." But somehow, we do. **Life is hard, but God is faithful**, and God will not allow us to be tested beyond our strength.

But sometimes God's faithfulness is shown in how God *provides*. God always provides a way of escape when the testing comes. At precisely the moment when our backs are against the wall and there seems to be no way out, the God who parted the waters of the Red Sea will make a way for us to pass through to the other side. **Life is hard, but God is faithful.**

On the front end of our trials, God is keeping us from suffering more than we can bear — and on the back end, God is making a way of escape when the trial comes. **Life is hard, but God is faithful.**

It is true that we cannot fully understand what someone else is going through. We have to be careful about telling anyone that we know what it must be like. We do not know unless we have been there — and even then, we cannot know the uniqueness of each person's experience. But we must also acknowledge the other side. There is also a sense in which everyone's experience is the same. We all share a common humanity, and God has brought us together in community that we might gain strength and support from others who are struggling through life. The rain falls on the just and the unjust. We all know what it is like to be tested — and we all know what it is like to fail. Our experiences may not be identical, but there is enough common humanity in all of us that enables us to identify with one another. **Life is hard, but God is faithful.**

Several years ago, Sylvia and I ran into a young woman whom I did not recognize at the time, but later remembered. She had seen my Erskine Seminary sweatshirt and asked me if I had a connection with Erskine. That opened up a conversation that reminded us both how we knew each other. Her husband had been a student at Erskine. I asked her about him and she told me that some time ago he had decided to transfer from Erskine to New Orleans Baptist Theological Seminary to complete his degree there. So, they both gave up their jobs, sold their house, packed all their belongings and moved to New Orleans along with their two preschool children so he could enroll in seminary there. Two months later, Hurricane Katrina ripped through New Orleans, devastating the city and temporarily shutting down the seminary. They packed up again and headed back to the Upstate where their family was so they could re-group and figure out what to do next.

Shortly after coming back home, their healthy preschool daughter developed a very rare, incurable brain disease known as Batten's Disease. One day she was the picture of health, running and playing and saying her ABC's as a normal four-year-old would do. Within a very short period of time, she was unable to walk or talk. At that time, the little girl was losing her vision and would eventually become totally blind before she would be reduced to a vegetative state and die. Because that precious little girl required around-the-clock care, her daddy had given up his plan to finish seminary for what he considered an even higher calling. Every day he stayed home with his helpless daughter, giving her the tender care she needed while her mother worked as a nurse at Greenville Memorial Hospital. I cannot tell you how our hearts broke that day as we listened to her tell the story. She seemed so together as she told how God had taken care of them, provided for their needs, given them strength for their trials and peace in their sorrow. There was a remarkable, quiet strength about her.

Not knowing what to say, but feeling like I needed to say something, I stumbled all over my words and said to her something like this: "I cannot imagine what this is like for you and your family and I am so sorry you are having to go through this experience." As I listened to her describe her situation, I felt so ashamed of how I complain about the trials of my life, which pale in comparison to hers. But I will never forget what she said or how she said it.

"We all have our trials. And I am sure that your trials are as serious to you as ours are to us. **Life is hard, but God is faithful,** and He will not allow us to be tested beyond our strength."

I walked away from that conversation sure that I had seen and heard a sermon far more compelling than any explanation I could have found in any of my books. Now that you are actually here and I am not having to look at empty pews and imagine who you are, I know I do not have to tell you that life is hard. Even though your situation may not seem as grim as the one that young family was facing with such courage, whatever you are going through, your trial may be as serious and threatening to you as theirs was to them. We are all struggling through life, facing trials that are different in their particularities, but common to us all. I do not have to tell you that life is hard, but I may need to remind you today that God is faithful. God will not let you be tested beyond your strength. **Life is hard, but God is faithful.**

With the testing, God will make a way where there seems to be no way. **Life is hard, but God is faithful.**

As surely as God parted the waters of the Red Sea, God will give you a way of escape in your trials. **Life is hard, but God is faithful.**

You may not feel like you can make it another day, but God will see you through all the way to the other side. **Life is hard, but God is faithful.**

As surely as the Israelites were in bondage, you may feel oppressed by the circumstances of your life — but just as God delivered them, God will deliver you. **Life is hard, but God is faithful.**

You may be in the wilderness now, but God is leading you into the land of promise. **Life is hard, but God is faithful.**

You may be tired and hungry and weak from the testings of your life, but God will give you enough food and nourishment and strength to make it another day. **Life is hard, but God is faithful.**

You may feel like you're all alone, but look around — God has surrounded you with people who are going through similar trials to support you along the way. **Life is hard, but God is faithful.**

Life is hard, but God is faithful.

Life is hard, but God is faithful.

Making Peace with Our Past and Our Future

MICAH 5:2-5A

> ^{2} *But you, O Bethlehem of Ephrathah,*
> *who are one of the little clans of Judah,*
> *from you shall come forth for me*
> *one who is to rule in Israel,*
> *whose origin is from of old,*
> *from ancient days.*
> ^{3} *Therefore he shall give them up until the time*
> *when she who is in labor has brought forth;*
> *then the rest of his kindred shall return*
> *to the people of Israel.*
> ^{4} *And he shall stand and feed his flock in the strength of the Lord,*
> *in the majesty of the name of the Lord his God.*
> *And they shall live secure, for now he shall be great*
> *to the ends of the earth;*
> ^{5} *and he shall be the one of peace.*

Many of us struggle to make peace with our past. Something was said or something was done, people were hurt and relationships were broken. Somewhere along the way, we let someone down. We disappointed ourselves, we disappointed the people we love the most, and we disappointed God — and some of us live with some measure of regret and guilt over what we have done. Or perhaps, some of us were the victims of *other* people's wrongdoings. We grew up in a dysfunctional family. We were abused or neglected by someone we trusted. Some of us were hurt or betrayed by someone in the church, or by the church itself. We were hurt, physically or emotionally, because someone was careless or reckless. And we carry around with us wherever we go some measure of unresolved bitterness or resentment. Many of us are trying to make peace with our past.

And, ironically, the very occasions that are supposed to bring the most peace to our lives can actually make peace seem even more elusive. Mother's Day, Father's Day, birthdays, and anniversaries are supposed to be occasions for celebration. The Advent/Christmas season is supposed to be the season of peace, goodwill to all people. But many of us resonate with at least one verse of Longfellow's poem:

> *And in despair, I bowed my head:*
> *"There is no peace on earth," I said.*
> *"For hate is strong and mocks the song*
> *Of peace on earth, goodwill to men."*[15]

In fact, some of us dread the month of December when we start getting all those picture-perfect, festive Christmas cards in the mail, picturing happy individuals and perfect families gathered around the Christmas tree in their perfect houses, dressed in their designer red and green clothes, wearing their Santa hats, with the family pet, wearing a red bandana, posing perfectly at their feet or in their arms. Of course,

---

15 Excerpt from *I Heard the Bells on Christmas Day*, by Henry W. Longfellow. Irmscher, Christoph. *Longfellow Redux*. Urbana: University of Illinois Press, 2006, 293.

with the prominence and prevalence of social media, we do not have to wait until December to see all the idyllic photos and videos and posts. When some of us look at those perfect pictures, we wonder why our lives and our families cannot look like that.

But that's just it. In some cases, *their* lives are not like that either — really. If being a pastor has taught me nothing else, it has taught me that most people have their own brokenness — and some people are just better at covering it up than others. Now that is not to say that there aren't some extraordinary people and families out there whose lives really are together. But not too many people and families are as perfect as their Christmas cards and Facebook posts would lead you to believe.

My brother, David, now has custody of a family portrait of my parents, my two brothers, and me that was once displayed prominently in the house in which we grew up. It is a touching scene. There we were all together in the same room at the same time, clean, dressed up, well-groomed, with the most peaceful expressions on our faces. It looks like a Norman Rockwell painting of an all-American family. It truly was a Kodak moment. You would never know by looking at that beautiful portrait that, just before the snapshot was taken, my father had to break up a fist fight between my two older brothers. Howell was making fun of David because the photographer had asked David to stand on a block to make him appear to be taller than he really was — and the fight was on. Howell was already in a bad mood because he had a date that night and didn't want to be there in the first place. I refused to smile because I didn't want my braces to show, and I only had on one shoe. We couldn't find the other one (although I have my suspicions as to who may have hidden it). Daddy was threatening us all the way, and Mother was praying that we would get through the appointment without any serious injuries.

After the photos were taken, I limped out with one shoe on and one shoe off and watched as David and Howell came to blows in the parking lot, while Daddy broke up their fight and Mother kept praying. But at the split second when the photograph was taken, we were the picture of bliss. And when you look at that family portrait, you don't see what happened before or after the picture was taken.

Our lives on the inside are not as peaceful as they might appear on the outside. We live in this moment with no way to undo the past or control the future. And that is why peace is so hard to come by. Some of us are trying to make peace with our past, with what has already happened. But some of us are trying to make peace with our future. At least with the past, we know what we are trying to get over. It is history. And it is done. But with the future comes uncertainty. We do not know what the future holds. There is no way for us to predict how our lives will unfold, what other people close to us will do with their lives that will impact ours. And we cannot see past this moment, how it will all turn out. And for some of us, the anxiety and fear almost take our breath away.

Just beyond the edges of this scene are the realities of death or divorce that will leave some of us with an empty chair around the family table at Christmas, or a stocking somewhere that stays folded in the box. And it will remain to be seen how or even if we will be able to put our lives back together. Some of us have lost a job and wonder how or if we will ever finish paying for the gifts around our tree. Some of us have family members who have broken our hearts by the choices they've made, and we try not to even think about what could happen to them. Some of us are limited by poor health and we are afraid of what will happen to us when we can no longer take care of ourselves. Some of us are wondering if this might be the last special occasion (birthday, anniversary, Christmas, family gathering) for us or for someone we love.

Some of us are trying to make peace with our past — and others of us are trying to make peace with our future. But all of us, in one way or another, are seeking peace. If we are seeking peace from our past, then our enemy may be guilt or pain. If we are seeking peace with our future, then our enemy may be anxiety or fear. But whatever the enemy, one of the most basic longings of the human soul is the longing for peace.

The prophet Micah was sent by God to promise peace to the people of Judah. There is no way to know what the exact historical circumstances were, but the people to whom this prophecy was addressed were in some kind of a miserable and desperate situation. From the context in chapter 4, we learn that they were under some kind of siege, and their leader was suffering insulting indignities at the hands of their foes. So, the promise came that God would send a deliverer who would be even more powerful than king David had been. Micah's prophecy added fuel to the messianic fires that, by that time, had begun to spread. By that time, there was already a widespread belief that God would send a divine deliverer, born of a woman — that is, fully human — who would inaugurate a new era of prosperity and peace. And all of these elements were present in our text from Micah's prophecy. The Messiah would come from God, would be of old, from ancient of days. The *deliverer* would be born of a woman, who, in labor, would deliver *him*. And when the Messiah would finally come, he would bring peace.

The biblical notion of peace is much deeper and richer than the mere absence of conflict. *Shalom*, the Hebrew word for peace, is far more than an outward, superficial prosperity. It is wellness and wholeness from the inside out. It is security and well-being. It is complete, harmonious unity with God and with others. Eight centuries before the birth of Jesus, the prophet Micah promised that the coming Messiah would bring that kind of peace. That promise would be personified in a king unlike any king they had known before. Their new ruler would come not from Jerusalem, but from Bethlehem, where King David had been born — not from prominence, but from obscurity; not as a warrior who would lead his army, but as a shepherd who would feed his flock. And the whole reason we gather to worship Sunday after Sunday is that we believe that promise has been fulfilled in Jesus Christ, who came to bring the kind of peace that we cannot produce ourselves — not by eliminating the brokenness of our lives and our world, but by redeeming it.

On our behalf, Jesus made peace with our past. The good news of the gospel is that, in the Jesus of history, God did for us what we could not do for ourselves. By His life, death, and resurrection, the historical Jesus "took our sins and our sorrows and made them His very own."[16] He soaked them up in Himself and robbed them of their destructive power.

But our faith in Jesus is not just a celebration of the Jesus of history. It is also about our anticipation of what Jesus will do in the future — when everything that has ever been wrong will be made right; when, in the words of Micah in the previous chapter, "swords will be beaten into plowshares and spears into pruning hooks, when nation will no longer lift up sword against nation, neither shall they learn of war anymore, but they shall all sit under their own vines and under their own fig trees, and no one shall make them afraid" (4:3-4); when at last God will see this world to sleep with "the sweet amen of peace."[17] The invitation of the gospel is for us to trust not just our past but our future to the God who has been made known to us in Jesus Christ.

We cannot undo what has been done in the past. We cannot remove the consequences of sinful behavior by our own efforts, however hard we try. And we cannot control so much of what *will* be done in the future either. The future is as *uncertain* as the past is *certain*. And so, as we look *back*, we constantly battle the enemies of guilt and pain, bitterness and resentment — and as we look *ahead*, we constantly battle the enemies of fear and anxiety, helplessness and uncertainty. But if we believe that

---

16 Charles H. Gabriel. *I Stand Amazed in the Presence.* Public domain.
17 Ernest W. Shurtleff. *Lead On, O King Eternal.* Public domain.

God is not an enemy whose favor we must win, but a Friend whose grace we can trust;[18] if we believe that God is for us and not against us; if we believe that God can be trusted to do for us what we cannot do for ourselves; and if we believe the Messiah who was born in Bethlehem long ago can be born in us today, then surely we can trust our past and our future to Him. Whether we are trying to make peace with our past, or peace with our future, what we are really trying to do is make peace with God. And the good news of the gospel is that, in Jesus Christ, God has made peace with us.

Gloria Gaither wrote:

When the whirlwinds of doubt churn their way into your soul,
When your world's reduced to ashes, leaving nothing firm and whole.
Take His peace.

There amidst the broken wreckage in the midnight of your day,
In the apex of the storm cloud, He's the quiet place to stay.
Take His peace.

When your mind gropes for answers to the questions that you face,
When your past comes back to haunt you and you need amazing grace,
Take His peace.

There's an answer beyond question, it's the truth for which you yearn:
There's forgiveness without merit, there's a love you need not earn.
Take His peace, take His peace, take His peace.[19]

---

18 Charles E. Poole. *Don't Cry Past Tuesday: Hopeful Words for Difficult Days* (Macon, Georgia: Smyth and Helwys Publishing, Inc., 1991), 22.
19 W.D. Cornell, W.G. Cooper, Gloria Gaither. *Take His Peace* (narration only). Copyright © 1978 Hanna Street Music (BMI) (adm. at CapitolCMGPublishing.com) All rights reserved. Used by permission.

I know how simplistic this may sound to those of us who are trying to make peace with our past and our future. I would not blame you at all if you were to think that I just don't understand the complexity or the magnitude of your situation. You may be thinking, "It's not as simple as just 'taking His peace.'" And you would be right. It's not easy to take God's peace when we are still holding on to the guilt and pain of the past, and the anxiety and fear of the future. It's not easy, as an act of our will, to let it all go and lay it all down. But the only way to receive God's peace is with empty hands. So it may not be *easy*, but it could be *simpler* than you ever dreamed it could be. If peace is a gift, then surely the only way to receive the gift is to let go of the guilt and pain of the past, the fear and anxiety of the future, and with empty hands receive the priceless gift of peace that Jesus came to give us.

Somebody's Gotta Go

MATTHEW 18:15-20

¹⁵ "If another member of the church sins against you, go and point out the fault when the two of you are alone. If the member listens to you, you have regained that one. ¹⁶ But if you are not listened to, take one or two others along with you, so that every word may be confirmed by the evidence of two or three witnesses. ¹⁷ If the member refuses to listen to them, tell it to the church; and if the offender refuses to listen even to the church, let such a one be to you as a Gentile and a tax collector. ¹⁸ Truly I tell you, whatever you bind on earth will be bound in heaven, and whatever you loose on earth will be loosed in heaven. ¹⁹ Again, truly I tell you, if two of you agree on earth about anything you ask, it will be done for you by my Father in heaven. ²⁰ For where two or three are gathered in my name, I am there among them."

Have you ever been in a relationship that had been so badly damaged that you felt like somebody had to go? Once when I was teaching a course at Erskine Seminary on "Christian Leadership and Church Administration," we were discussing some actual case studies that we were facing in our ministries, seeking to apply the course material to each of them. We had just finished a discussion on the five approaches to conflict resolution, and I asked the students to write about a conflict they had experienced in the church. Then we set aside some time in class to discuss a few of them. One of the students shared that, over the course of time, a feud had developed between two people in the church over the youth ministry. The conflict started out being about whether the youth should only go to Presbyterian-sponsored youth camps, or whether the youth minister should be free to choose whichever camp seemed to best meet the needs of the youth in the group. But the dispute escalated and became very personal — and at one point, one of them came to the youth minister and said, "I can't stay in this church as long as so-and-so is here. Somebody's gotta go. It's either him or me."

We discussed what was really going on in that exchange and what some of the underlying issues might have been. But we all concluded that when there is a stand-off or a stalemate between two people, especially two Christians in the same church, before somebody leaves, all attempts at reconciliation and restoration must be made. When two people have reached an impasse, somebody's gotta go ... to the other person. In the body of Christ, and in the family of God, it may be true that somebody's gotta go. But we do not have the luxury of giving up prematurely and going *away* from each other until we have first gone *toward* each other. We do not have the right to talk *about* each other until we have first talked *to* each other.

The New Testament describes the church as a family that shares a common meal around a common table. In the body of Christ, we not only eat family style, but we share life together family style. It is vitally important for us to find a way to work together as a family for the common good, while still celebrating our differences. That's the way the church is supposed to work. But let's face it: Sometimes that is not the way it is. Some of the worst behavior I have ever witnessed has been in the church. As Christians, though we have been saved from sin, we still battle our sinful nature. What appears to be a conflict over which youth camp to choose is often nothing more than a battle for control. Unfortunately and sadly, the church is not immune to conflicts that too often are more about ego than anything else.

The truth is that we not only learn how to share in families, but we also learn how to fight in families. That's how I learned how to fight — with my brothers! The worst disputes in society are usually among family members. Statistics show that an alarming number of murders each year take place within families. Regrettably, that is the case with the family of God as well — usually not murders — but just a few years ago, I heard of a church right here in Greenville in which a fist fight broke out during a church conference.

Sometimes churches are too quick to fight. But sometimes, churches don't know *how* to fight. Too many of us have been conditioned to believe that we should "leave well enough alone," that we should "let sleeping dogs lie." But some of those sleeping dogs wake up and bite. Some of us have been taught too well that "if we cannot say anything nice to somebody, we shouldn't say anything at all." Too many of us have been taught to "ignore it, and it will go away," only to learn the hard way that it does not. These are the lessons that many of us learned in our own families of origin and have brought with us into the family of God. Some church members are too quick to build walls, and too slow to build bridges. But sometimes, there are disputes that are important, disagreements that are really about substance and values and convictions.

Some people value purity more than unity. They would rather be right than keep the family together. But some people believe that keeping the family together is even more important than being right. The writer of Ecclesiastes observed that "there is a time break down and a time to build up … a time to embrace and a time to refrain from embracing, a time to seek and a time to lose, a time to keep and a time to cast away … a time to keep silence and a time to speak, a time to love and a time to hate, a time for war and a time for peace." The problem for most of us is knowing what time it is. When is it time to pull together? And when is it time to pull apart?

In the eighteenth chapter of Matthew, and especially in this text, Jesus emphasizes the value of Christian community. Regardless of what some of us have been conditioned to believe, our relationship with Christ is not a private matter. To be sure, there is a personal dimension to it — but the personal dimension can never be separated from the interpersonal dimension to it. There is something mystical and mysterious that happens when two or three people are gathered in the name of Christ. True community is either formed or embarrassingly malformed in the church. But in this passage, Jesus is promising to be with us when we are together with as few as two or three others who are seeking authentic community.

According to Jesus, this is the way conflict resolution is supposed to work. First, the victim is supposed to take the initiative in restoring the relationship with a brother or sister. "If your brother or sister sins against *you*," Jesus said, "it is *your* responsibility to go to that person to make it right." And it is right here that the process often breaks down. Many of us have been taught so well to just let things go that we pretend nothing has happened. It may be awkward being around that person, but it is better to be awkward than to have a fight. Or, instead, we may give the offender the cold shoulder. It would be impolite to tell the person what is wrong, so we just shun the person. If that doesn't work, we may passively or aggressively seek revenge — just let it leak out all over the place, embark on a private smear campaign[20] — all this instead of going straight to the person to work it out. If someone else has done *us* wrong, why should *we* be the ones to go to *him* or *her*? Why shouldn't *he* or *she* come to us? If somebody's gotta go, why do I have to be the one? Well, one practical reason is that *we* may actually be the

---

20 Barbara Brown Taylor. *The Seeds of Heaven: Sermons on the Gospel of Matthew* (Louisville: Westminster John Knox Press, 2004), 87.

ones who were wrong. When we go to a person to tell him or her what *we think* is wrong, if we are open to that person, we may discover that there is enough blame to go around, or that the whole conflict is one big misunderstanding. The best way to resolve a conflict is to admit that we, too, could be wrong.[21] Another practical reason is that some people will keep on taking advantage of us as long as they can. People cannot control our lives unless *we give them* control of us. Going to that person is refusing to give that person control over us.

Another way the process breaks down prematurely is that we often default to talking *about* people, rather than talking *to* them. If there is any sin in the church that can cause unrest and division, it is this — talking *about* people instead of talking *to* them. In my kind of work, I am often called upon to mediate disputes between people in the church, or in a family. And one of the first questions I have learned to ask is, "Have you talked to the person directly?" It is amazing to me how often the answer is "no." Sometimes the hurt can be healed by simply having an honest and timely conversation with the person who has sinned against you. If that works, then Jesus said, "You have gained your brother (or sister)" (Matthew 18:15). On the front end, before lines get drawn and walls get built, somebody's gotta go. Somebody's gotta take the initiative to put aside pride and ego for the good of the family of God, and somebody's gotta go to the person with whom there is an unresolved conflict. And that somebody may be you.

But, human nature being what it is, sometimes that step, by itself, is not enough. People become defensive, walls get constructed, people are more interested in winning than understanding, lines get drawn in the sand, people refuse to listen to one another, there are disputes over facts or shutdowns over emotions. And Jesus said, when that happens,

---

21 Ibid., 88.

it may be time to get other people involved. It is not yet time to give up. It is time to get help in resolving the conflict. Sometimes third parties can help you hear each other and understand each other. Sometimes somebody who is not involved in the dispute can mediate a productive conversation and help you listen beneath the words for the meanings. If the person who has sinned against you does not listen, then "take one or two others along with you." That would make two or three, total. And if that goes nowhere, it is still not permissible to give up on reconciliation. The relationship is so valuable and the tie that binds so important, that you may even have to take the matter to the church, or at least representatives of the larger church family. Do you see how valuable the relationships are in the church between brothers and sisters? It is not something from which you just walk away. Somebody may have to go eventually. Regrettably, some people, even in the church, have to part ways, but only after every possible attempt at reconciliation has been made.

If every attempt has been exhausted and still no restoration has taken place, then there may come a time when you have to let a person go. Sometimes people have to go, and sometimes, even in the church, they have to let go. Barbara Brown Taylor says, "The only thing worse than losing a brother or sister is pretending that you have not and letting that person fester in your midst like an untended wound."[22] When we deal with one another with integrity and follow the spirit of what Jesus has taught, when we have done all we know to do and it still has not been enough, then we have the promise of Christ that God will honor the outcome and Christ himself will be with us.

In talking to people who are in conflict, I find myself asking them often, "Have you done everything in your power to make this relationship work? Have you exhausted all the possibilities for restoration?

---

22 Barbara Brown Taylor, 85.

Have you done everything you believe God expects you to do? Have you left no stone unturned in your attempt to reconcile the broken relationship?" And if I hear them answer "yes" to those questions with great clarity, then I believe it is time for them to grieve that person and let him or her go. Once you have done all you can do, then there comes a time when you have to trust God to do what only God can do. It is not that you cannot continue to pray for that person or care for that person. But there comes a time when somebody's gotta go, and somebody's gotta *let* go.

After John Mark decided to leave Paul on their first mission trip and go back home prematurely, Paul decided not to take John Mark along the next time. We are not told how or if they tried to resolve the conflict, but we are told that they parted ways and may have ended up accomplishing more apart than they ever would have together. I have known of churches and denominations that have pulled apart, split right down the middle, over matters great and small. I have known of people who have agonized over a decision to leave a local church that they loved so much because it was doing more harm than good to stay. I have known of marriages that could not be saved despite the best efforts of one spouse or the other, and sometimes even both spouses.

And the point is that when as few as two or three people, or as many as thousands of people, are genuinely striving to honor the name of Christ, He has promised to be in their midst whether they stay together or pull apart. Sometimes somebody's gotta go. Somebody's gotta be the one to make the first move toward reconciliation. Restoration, harmony, and unity must always be the goal. But sometimes, after the first move and the second, and the third — when all options have been tried and every effort has been made, somebody's gotta *let* go — and then trust that the presence of the living Christ will be with *us* and with *them*, doing with all of us, together or apart, what only God can do.

Stand Up Straight
PROVERBS 11:3

The integrity of the upright guides them,
but the crookedness of the treacherous destroys them.

When I was young, my father drilled in me the importance of good posture. At the first or slightest sign that I was slumping my shoulders, he would say to me, "Stand up straight!" It was something that was drilled into *him* by *his* father. He placed a high value on good posture, and could not stand to see anyone slumped over or leaning to the right or to the left. And he never hesitated to call me on it — long after I grew up. In fact, not long before he died, we were looking at some family photographs, and he turned to me and asked, "Why is your head always leaning to the left?" At first it made me angry that he said that. But when I took a closer look at all the family photographs, he was right. My head *was* always leaning to the left. He made me so self-conscious that, before every photograph after that, I over-corrected, and now, in all the photographs, my head is always leaning to the right. I do not know why it is so hard for me to stand up straight. But I know I'm not the only one who has that problem.

Everywhere you turn in the book of Proverbs, the wisdom writer is telling us in so many words to "stand up straight," offering unsolicited advice on just about every subject imaginable, even how to have good posture — but not the kind of physical posture my father was always observing. The word often used in the book of Proverbs to describe moral and ethical posture is the word that is usually translated "upright."

In our text, the wisdom poet uses a common literary technique to make a point in the first line, and then to state the antithesis of that point in the second line:

> *The integrity of the upright guides them,*
> **but** *the crookedness of the treacherous destroys them.*

This poetic structure is designed to make the opposites clear, and the word translated "upright" simply means "straight." It is not just to be right, but it is to be up and right. It is to resist the destructive, crooked, and treacherous forces that would draw us to one side or the other. To be upright is not to droop or stoop or sink or slump to the forces that would pull us down. It is to be drawn upward, "pressing on the *upward* way" (as the old hymn says).[23] Rather than being pulled down, or to one side or the other, the upright person is always seeking the mind and heart of God, who is always above and beyond our highest thoughts. Speaking on behalf of God, the ancient prophet wrote, "For as the heavens are higher than the earth, so are my ways higher than your ways, and my thoughts than your thoughts" (Isaiah 55:9). The only way to be upright is to seek above all else the ways and thoughts of God, which are always infinitely higher than our own ways and thoughts. To be upright is to stretch, not to stoop. It is to take the high road, not the low road. It is to let God and God alone define who we are, what we do, how we think, and how we live.

And if there is ever a time when this word needs to be heard, it is now. In a world that is becoming increasingly polarized, the people of God are called to be upright, leaning not to one side or the other, but always being drawn and stretched upward. The only way to be upright in a crooked,

---

23 Johnson Oatman, Jr. *Higher Ground*. Public domain.

twisted world is not to look down to gain a righteous perspective, but to look up — not to look to one side or the other for answers, but to look above. The psalmist prayed to God, "To You I lift *up* my eyes, O You who are enthroned in the heavens" (Psalm 123:1)! In a culture that is constantly lowering and shifting its standards, the people of God are called to look upward for a higher righteousness that transcends any ideology we could ever construct.

It seems that every time we blink our eyes, we find ourselves in another election cycle. And obviously, if you vote, you are going to have to choose sides. But what I am talking about is not primarily the actual choice you make. It is primarily about the process by which you make the choice. It is about your *starting* point, not just your *ending* point. To be upright is to start not with some preconceived notions of the truth. It is to start not with our own agenda or ideology. To be upright is to start with God and God alone — the truth and justice, love and mercy of God, revealed in Jesus Christ. To be upright is to recognize that, compared to that standard, any choice we make will be an imperfect choice. In this fallen world, we will always be forced to choose between options, neither of which is completely satisfactory. So at every point, we must resist the temptation to put our faith in political and ideological constructions, however noble we may think they are.

And what is true of our political choices is true of *all* the moral and ethical choices we make in life. In our families, in our schools, in our churches and denominations, in our civic organizations, and in our workplaces, we are constantly being forced to align ourselves with people and groups and positions that are intrinsically flawed. We are always being asked to make decisions and choose between options that are not ideal. There may be good reasons to take one position, and reasons that are just as good to take the opposite position. One option may be a bad choice, and another option may be just as bad for a different reason. The choices we make are profoundly important, and the stakes are high. But being upright is not just about the choices we make; it is about the process by which we make them.

And if our starting point is anything or anyone other than God, revealed in Jesus Christ, if we are defined by any affiliation other than our relationship with Him, then we are only revealing the idols we worship. Part of the reason why some people *demonize* people on the *other* side is because they have *idolized* people on *their* side. They have not learned to distinguish between their ways and the ways of God. The point is that if we expect any person or party or organization or ideology to completely reflect the nature and character of God, then we will be sadly disappointed. As people of God, we must always remember that all candidates are flawed, all ideologies are incomplete, all organizations are impure, all party platforms are compromises, and all voters (including ourselves) have blind spots, prejudices, biases, and flaws — "sinful beyond measure," as Paul said to the Romans (Romans 7:13).

To be upright is not necessarily to declare one side completely right and the other completely wrong, but to declare that *both* sides are broken and *neither* side is completely right on every issue. Now that does not mean that we should not choose sides. It is important for the people of God to take a stand. So we sign petitions, join organizations, get involved in the community, and seek to influence the political process based on the information we have — but we always remember that the issues we face are often immensely complex, and our knowledge is always incomplete. As sinful human beings, we contribute to the infection of the very systems we deplore. Our understanding of the truth of God is always limited and incomplete. So those who are upright take their stands, make their choices, and vote their consciences, but they do so with great humility, realizing that God's ways and thoughts are infinitely beyond our ability to comprehend. That is why I believe with every fiber of my being that what honors God even more than the positions we take on any given issue is the genuine desire of our hearts to seek God's way first, and to know and do God's will above all else.

We live in a world in which the lines have been drawn, the litmus tests have been established, the buzz words have been identified, and the labels have been assigned — and the people of God are constantly being forced to choose sides and take positions that will win them the favor of one side and invite the scorn of the other side, sometimes not stopping even for a moment to consider how God is above it all.

I am longing and praying and working for the day when we, as God's people:

- Become more concerned about being on God's side than we are about proving that God is on our side.
- Can acknowledge that the truth of God cannot be contained by any ideology or label.
- Are as quick to acknowledge our own blind spots and sins as we are to acknowledge the blind spots and sins of those who disagree with us.
- Get out of our echo chambers long enough to acknowledge that there is often some measure of truth on both sides.
- Quit letting ideologues on either side define who we are or what we do.
- Refuse to let the gravitational forces of our culture pull us downward.

I long for the day when we stand up straight, being drawn upward to a God who will not be defined by our political positions or contained by our theological constructions, a God whose truth is infinitely higher than our perception of it, a God whose righteousness is always more than our highest or noblest intentions.

Now some may hear this as an attempt to straddle the fence and have it both ways. But, as I understand it, to be upright is not to have it *both* ways. It is to have it *neither* way. It is to seek *another* way, a *higher* way, a *better* way — God's way, even when God's way means parting company with people whose approval we would do almost anything to get. To be upright is not to *straddle* the fence; it is to *climb* the fence, being drawn upward, rising above it all, scaling the utmost height, pressing on the upward way, seeking the mind and heart of God above all else.

And so I tell you what my father told me, "Stand up straight." Be upright. Look not to one side or the other, but look above. Open your mind and heart above all else to the will and way of God. Saturate your heart with the truth of God revealed in Scripture and personified in Jesus the Christ. Press on toward the goal for the prize of the heavenly call of God in Christ Jesus" (Philippians 3:14). And be sure you know, that if you follow in His ways and obey Him, you will be in good company. You may have to part company with people who are convinced that God is on *their* side. But you will be in the company of One who alone can bring you to *God's* own side. As it turned out, for Jesus, the only way to be upright was on a cross — crucified by those who were convinced that God was on their side. On the cross, Jesus was lifted high above those who put Him there, praying for their forgiveness, dying *upright* as He had lived.

The Economy of God
AMOS 6:1A, 4-7; 1 TIMOTHY 6:6-19; LUKE 16:19-31

¹ Alas for those who are at ease in Zion …

⁴ Alas for those who lie on beds of ivory,
and lounge on their couches,
and eat lambs from the flock,
and calves from the stall;
⁵ who sing idle songs to the sound of the harp,
and like David improvise on instruments of music;
⁶ who drink wine from bowls,
and anoint themselves with the finest oils,
but are not grieved over the ruin of Joseph!
⁷ Therefore they shall now be the first to go into exile,
and the revelry of the loungers shall pass away.
— Amos 6:1a, 4-7

¹⁹ "There was a rich man who was dressed in purple and fine linen and who feasted sumptuously every day. ²⁰ And at his gate lay a poor man named Lazarus, covered with sores, ²¹ who longed to satisfy his hunger with what fell from the rich man's table; even the dogs would come and lick his sores. ²² The poor man died and was carried away by the angels to be with Abraham. The rich man also died and was buried. ²³ In Hades, where he was being tormented, he looked up and saw Abraham

far away with Lazarus by his side. ²⁴ *He called out, 'Father Abraham, have mercy on me, and send Lazarus to dip the tip of his finger in water and cool my tongue; for I am in agony in these flames.'* ²⁵ *But Abraham said, 'Child, remember that during your lifetime you received your good things, and Lazarus in like manner evil things; but now he is comforted here, and you are in agony.* ²⁶ *Besides all this, between you and us a great chasm has been fixed, so that those who might want to pass from here to you cannot do so, and no one can cross from there to us.'* ²⁷ *He said, 'Then, father, I beg you to send him to my father's house —* ²⁸ *for I have five brothers — that he may warn them, so that they will not also come into this place of torment.'* ²⁹ *Abraham replied, 'They have Moses and the prophets; they should listen to them.'* ³⁰ *He said, 'No, father Abraham; but if someone goes to them from the dead, they will repent.'* ³¹ *He said to him, 'If they do not listen to Moses and the prophets, neither will they be convinced even if someone rises from the dead.'" — Luke 16:19-31*

⁶ Of course, there is great gain in godliness combined with contentment; ⁷ *for we brought nothing into the world, so that we can take nothing out of it;* ⁸ *but if we have food and clothing, we will be content with these.* ⁹ *But those who want to be rich fall into temptation and are trapped by many senseless and harmful desires that plunge people into ruin and destruction.* ¹⁰ *For the love of money is a root of all kinds of evil, and in their eagerness to be rich some have wandered away from the faith and pierced themselves with many pains.* ¹¹ *But as for you, man of God, shun all this; pursue righteousness, godliness, faith, love, endurance, gentleness.* ¹² *Fight the good fight of the faith; take hold of the eternal life, to which you were called and for which you made* *the good confession in the presence of many witnesses. *¹³* In the presence of God, who gives life to all things, and of Christ Jesus, who in his testimony before Pontius Pilate made the good confession, I charge you *¹⁴* to keep the commandment without spot or blame until the manifestation of our Lord Jesus Christ, *¹⁵* which he will bring about at the right time — he who is the blessed and only Sovereign, the King of kings and Lord of lords. *¹⁶* It is he alone who has immortality and dwells in unapproachable light, whom no one has ever seen or can see; to him be honor and eternal dominion. Amen. *¹⁷* As for those who in the present age are rich, command them not to be haughty, or to set their hopes on the uncertainty of riches, but rather on God who richly provides us with everything for our enjoyment. *¹⁸* They are to do good, to be rich in good works, generous, and ready to share, *¹⁹* thus storing up for themselves the treasure of a good foundation for the future, so that they may take hold of the life that really is life. — 1 Timothy 6:6-19*

My good friend and former pastor, Marshall Sargent, loved to tell the story of the time when he was in seminary and one of his fellow students asked his preaching professor how many points a sermon should have. The wise professor replied, "At least one." Every sermon should have at least one point. But somewhere along the way, it became customary for preachers to have three points. I don't know exactly how or when that trend got started — but for a long time, that was kind of the norm. It still is in some circles. There would be an introduction, three points (and it would be even better if the points were alliterated or rhymed), and a conclusion, which was usually a poem. But I have never been able to preach that way. Maybe it was the way I was taught in seminary, or maybe it is just the way I think. But it just doesn't come naturally for me to have multiple points in the same sermon. I have always thought I would be doing well if I could make just one point — and sometimes, I can't even seem to do that. But since the lectionary calls for us to consider several passages of Scripture, and I was drawn to three of them, I thought I would take a stab at developing a three-point sermon, one point from each passage. I'm not sure I can pull this off, but let's see.

Long ago in a far-away place, the prophet Amos warned the people in an affluent society not to be "at ease in Zion" (Amos 6:1). And when we hear his vivid description of that time and place, it doesn't sound so long ago or far away. During the long and peaceful reign of Jeroboam II in the eighth century BC, the northern kingdom of Israel attained a height of territorial expansion and national prosperity never again reached. And many Israelites saw their wealth and prosperity as signs of God's blessing. There was a popular view, especially among the rich, that God blesses the righteous and punishes the sinful. And they had no trouble finding passages of Scripture to back up their views. For example, there was the passage in Deuteronomy 28 that promises fertility, prosperity, and victory in war to those who obey the Lord. Sprinkled throughout the Old Testament are those passages like the one in Psalm 1 that make it clear that the Lord watches over the way of the righteous, but the way of the wicked will perish. Those who obeyed God were blessed and those who did not were condemned.

That kind of theology worked out nicely for them on two counts. It not only allowed the rich to enjoy their riches, but it also allowed them to walk past the poor beggars in their streets without getting too distracted or feeling too guilty. But the prophet Amos would not allow them to be "at ease in Zion." There was another side to Israel's affluence. There always is another side to wealth. Though it was the best of times for some, it was the worst of times for others. The rich were getting richer and the poor were getting poorer. And many believed that was the way God distinguished between the righteous and the sinful.

It is called "health and wealth theology" and you do not need me to tell you that it is still around. To be sure, if you are looking for a Scriptural justification for wealth, you can find it easily enough. But you have to overlook other Scriptures to do so. And we are all very selective when it comes to Scripture and very good at picking and choosing the passages that back up our views and our ways of life. Of course, the Hebrew Scriptures are filled with passages that went the other way. For example, on their way to Deuteronomy 28, the people would have had to pass right by the passage in Deuteronomy 15:11 that says: "Open your hand to the poor and needy neighbor in your land." And then there is the verse in Proverbs 14:31: "Those who oppress the poor insult their Maker, but those who are kind to the needy honor Him." Passages like those made it clear that, far from *judging* the poor, God actually identified with them. To walk past a beggar, in that sense, was to walk past God. Amos didn't mince any words:

> *Alas for those who lie on beds of ivory, and lounge on their couches, and eat lambs from the flock, and calves from the stall; who sing idle songs to the sound of the harp, and like David improvise on instruments of music; who drink wine from bowls, and anoint themselves with the finest oils, but are not grieved over the ruin of Joseph!*

Someone has said that the word of God comforts the disturbed and disturbs the comfortable. It seems that Amos's message would have done both. It would have comforted those who were poor, but it would have disturbed those who were rich. The problem with the rich was not their possessions; it was that they were so much "at ease" with their affluence that they did not see the needy all around them. Rather than prompting them to reach out to the poor, their possessions had insulated them from the poor. They were out of touch with and undisturbed by the ruin of their own country. Their wealth had become the end, the ultimate, rather than a means to a greater end. Their possessions had begun to possess them. They had become hardened, calloused, and cavalier about the plight of those who had no wealth or power. But, speaking on behalf of God, Amos came to tell them that, **in God's economy, what matters most is not what we *have*, but what we *grieve*.**

The people of Israel sound like the rich man who had made a name for himself in his world, but, in the story Jesus told, had no name. For this rich man, life was a daily banquet at a bounteous table, his abundance spilling over onto the floor. He was draped in robes of royalty over fine undergarments. Nothing about him even hinted of need. The poor man, on the other hand, might have been nameless in his world — but in Jesus's story, he had a name. His name was Lazarus, which means "God helps." Jesus pictured Lazarus squatting or lying among the dogs that licked his sores at the gate of the rich man's house: gaunt, hollow-eyed, and famished — turned toward the rich man's house with the stare of death upon his face, desiring only the crumbs that might have fallen from the rich man's table. Both men died (which is a point not to be overlooked, for death is no respecter of persons or status). Death is the great equalizer and it has a way of coming down every street and knocking on every door. After death, the status of each man was exactly and unalterably reversed. Lazarus was seated at the messianic banquet table as an honored guest with Abraham — and the rich man became the beggar, lying in anguish in the flames of Hades. Moreover, just as there had been in life, there was in death a great chasm between the two. This is such a disturbing story any way you look at it, with such graphic images and descriptive language — the oozing sores, the slobbering dogs, the place of torment, the great chasm, and the finality of it all. This rich man liked the distance between him and Lazarus when it was his own doing — but now that the tables had turned and Lazarus had something he wanted, he was the one in distress. Even on the far side of the grave, the rich man still saw Lazarus as something less than a fellow human being. He thought of Lazarus as his water boy, Abraham's gofer, someone to fetch water and take messages. "Send Lazarus to me with some water," he said. But, cradling Lazarus in his bosom, Father Abraham set him straight. The rich man's days of getting other people to do his bidding were over. Furthermore, there would be no special messages brought back from the dead for his brothers. His brothers already had in their Scriptures all the truth and guidance they needed. They already had the law of Moses that commanded them to take care of the poor, and they already had the prophets like Amos who had warned them about being at ease in Zion — and if that was not enough to get their attention, then no ghost was going to get it either. It is not the persuasiveness of the sign that makes people obedient; it is the openness of their hearts to the word and will of God.[24]

What makes this such a disturbing story is that once we get into this story, we can't get out of it alive. It is a story about many of us loving the things we can get for ourselves better than we love the things God wants to give us. We become satisfied with linen suits and sumptuous feasts when God wants to give us the kingdom. We are content to live in a world with beggars and gofers when God wants to give us brothers and sisters. We are happy to get by with the parts of the Bible that back up our own ways of life when God wants to give us a new life altogether.

---

24 Barbara Brown Taylor. *Bread of Angels* (Cambridge, Massachusetts: Cowley Publications, 1999), 109-113.

We are victims of our own way of life. When we succeed in cutting ourselves off from each other, when we learn how to live with the misery of other people by convincing ourselves that they deserve it, when we defend our own good fortune as God's blessing and decline to see how our lives are quilted together with all other lives, then we are the losers — and not primarily because of what God will do to us, but because of what we have done to ourselves. Who do you think fixed that chasm in the story? Was it God or the rich man? Sometimes I think the worst thing we ever have to fear is that God will give us exactly what we want. This is a disturbing story, no doubt about it. But there is one good feature of this story: it is not over yet. For the rich man, yes — but not for us because we're still here, at least for now, and we have what Father Abraham would not give the five brothers. In addition to the law and the prophets, we *do* have One who has risen from the dead to convince us that, **in God's economy, what matters most is not what we *have*, but what we *give*.**

Paul certainly realized what a strangled hold our possessions can have on us. After giving his son in the faith guidance in matters of church administration, and opposing false teachers in the church, Paul closes his first letter to young Timothy by warning him not to be seduced by this world and the things in it: "For we brought nothing into the world, so that we can take nothing out of it" (1 Timothy 6:7). There is a great danger in being too much at ease and too content with what we have. Contentment in life must always be accompanied and tempered by godliness. Instead of buying into the bankrupt value system of this world, aim higher. Aim at righteousness and godliness, faith and love, steadfastness and gentleness. There is more than one way to measure wealth. Instead of being rich in things, be rich in good deeds. For it is not *money* that is the root of all kinds of evil. It is the *love* of money. In this passage, Paul reminds Timothy and all of us that, **in God's**

economy, what matters most is not what we *have*, but what we *love*.

So we have come to the end of the sermon and it's time to see how well I communicated and how well you listened. Did you pick up on all three points? In God's economy, what matters most is:

(1) not what we *have*, but what we *grieve;*
(2) not what we *have*, but what we *give;*
(3) not what we *have*, but what we *love.*

If you got that much, you are doing well. But here's the test for the advanced listeners. How many points did this sermon *really* have? Actually, these three points are really different ways of making the same point: **in the economy of God, what matters most is not what we *have*, but *Who* has *us*.** See, I can't come up with a three-point sermon even when I try. The other three points are folded into that single point. For when we give ourselves to Christ and surrender to His Lordship, we will make it our aim to grieve what He grieves, give as He gives, and love as He loves. Amen.

The Energy of Righteousness

JOHN 2:13-22

> ¹³ *The Passover of the Jews was near, and Jesus went up to Jerusalem.* ¹⁴ *In the temple he found people selling cattle, sheep, and doves, and the money changers seated at their tables.* ¹⁵ *Making a whip of cords, he drove all of them out of the temple, both the sheep and the cattle. He also poured out the coins of the money changers and overturned their tables.* ¹⁶ *He told those who were selling the doves, "Take these things out of here! Stop making my Father's house a marketplace!"* ¹⁷ *His disciples remembered that it was written, "Zeal for your house will consume me."* ¹⁸ *The Jews then said to him, "What sign can you show us for doing this?"* ¹⁹ *Jesus answered them, "Destroy this temple, and in three days I will raise it up."* ²⁰ *The Jews then said, "This temple has been under construction for forty-six years, and will you raise it up in three days?"* ²¹ *But he was speaking of the temple of his body.* ²² *After he was raised from the dead, his disciples remembered that he had said this; and they believed the scripture and the word that Jesus had spoken.*

Some people have what we call "anger issues." And it has been my experience that people who have anger issues get really angry when you tell them they have anger issues. They tend to lack self-awareness and always blame other people for "making" them angry. But there is a sense in which no one can *make* you angry. We *choose* to be angry. And what we *choose* to be angry about will speak volumes about who we are. Some people are just angry people, and they do not even think of themselves that way. They move from job to job, from church to church, from relationship to relationship every time they get angry. Rather than learning how to deal with anger in a healthy way, they recycle their unresolved anger everywhere they go. They have so much anger inside that every straw is a straw that breaks the camel's back.

In my counseling courses in seminary, my professor taught us to pay careful attention to the emotion of anger, and always be willing to ask the probing question: "What is this anger really about?" So let's say a husband gets angry with his wife and says it is because she is wrong, when in fact, he is really angry because she is right. She has touched a nerve and has spoken a truth about him that he is unwilling to admit. So he gets defensive, puts up his guard, makes counter charges against her, goes into a rage or shuts down the conversation not because she is wrong, but because she is right. The truth usually makes us angry before it makes us free.[25] Or perhaps the wife has had a horrible day at work, and gets angry at her husband because he has not folded the laundry. But what she is really angry about is what happened at work. So she takes it out on the nearest person or the pet or the innocent person at the check-out counter. Sometimes anger is not about the presenting issue, but is much deeper. And sometimes anger is misplaced, directed toward the wrong person, or even turned inward on ourselves. Our anger is a window into our souls. It exposes who we are in terms of our character and personality. No one wants to be around an angry person because anger can be a very destructive emotion. But anger can also be our friend. It is an emotion that *can* energize us to do what we most need

---

25 Emmanuel McCall. *The Black Christian Experience* (Nashville: Broadman Press, 1972), 103.

to do, but may not have the strength to do otherwise. It is *always* an emotion that should be *controlled*, but it is *not* always an emotion that should be *avoided*. Paul wrote, "Be angry, but do not sin" (Ephesians 4:26a). There is a healthy way for us to express anger, and sometimes anger is the only emotion that will energize us to do what is right. I know people who have suppressed anger through the years and have turned their anger inward. I know people who couldn't grieve the death of a relationship until they became angry enough to let the person go. I know people who really needed to make a change at work or at home or even in the church, but could not make the change until they became angry enough. Anger is not always, but certainly can be, the energy of righteousness.

This passage from John's Gospel shows that anger was, for Jesus, the energy of righteousness — and just as our anger reveals who *we* are, Jesus's anger revealed who He was. Normally, we picture Jesus as being a docile, meek, mild, gentle Savior. We picture Him healing people, blessing children, forgiving sinners, teaching love and kindness. But in our text, we get a rare glimpse of another side of Jesus's personality. It is an event we euphemistically refer to as "the cleansing of the temple." We picture Jesus entering the temple to sanitize the place and give it a thorough cleaning. But of course, that is not exactly what happened. In Matthew, Mark, and Luke, the so-called "cleansing of the temple" takes place just five days before Jesus was crucified. But in John's Gospel, it takes place at the very beginning of Jesus's public ministry, setting the tone and stage for all that will follow. It is not the only time we see Him angry, but it certainly is the most dramatic display of His anger. If you take a step back and look at Jesus's most offensive language and behavior, you will notice that it is always directed toward religious people. Jesus could deal kindly with the prostitutes and corrupt tax collectors. He could show compassion and mercy to adulterers and people considered "unclean." But one category of people that riled Him up was pretentious, self-righteous, corrupt religious people. And in the face of that kind of corruption, Jesus's anger became for Him the energy of righteousness.

The temple was supposed to be the house of God. It was supposed to be a sacred place. I remember when I was just a preschooler growing up at Central Baptist Church in Mrs. Nell's Beginner's Class. When we got just a little rowdy, as preschoolers are prone to do, Mrs. Nell would very quietly and calmly put the fear of God in us as she softly sang, "In God's house be very quiet." And it was almost like we fell into a trance as a holy hush swept across the room. I was taught at a very early age that God's house is different. It does not look like any other house. We do not do in here what we do everywhere else. We don't yell and scream and run in God's house. We were taught that God's house is different from all the other places of our lives.

In the Old Testament, the covenant people were always building monuments, setting up markers, and even changing the names of certain places where they met God and where God met them. It was not so they could worship the place, but so that they could mark the place and remember the spot where the transcendent God had met them. At first, God's homes were located in tents of meeting, tabernacles, as they were called — showing that God was mobile and God's presence could not be limited or confined to any one location. But eventually, in the days of Solomon, God's people built a more permanent dwelling place, the temple, an elaborate structure which came to be known as the house of God. There was always the understanding that God's presence was not *restricted* to that place, but there was always the belief that the temple was the *unique* place of God's presence. Four centuries after the temple was built, the Babylonian army destroyed it — and some seventy years after that date, the temple was re-built and re-dedicated. And it remained essentially as it was for centuries until the great rebuilding program of King Herod, which began around 20 BC.

The setting for the passage we have read from John's Gospel was some forty-six years after Herod's massive rebuilding program had begun. It was the Passover season, and by this time, there was a highly developed sacrificial system in place. For the convenience of the worshipers, animals were sold for sacrifice right there in the temple complex. Roman money was changed into Jewish money to pay the temple tax. And apparently, the exchange of money for a fee, especially during the busy season of Passover, lent itself to abuse. People were figuring out how to use the system to make a profit at the expense of the poor and the pious, and it was all happening right there in God's house. But Jesus would not stand for it. He made a whip of cords and drove the animals and the people out of the temple. He poured out the coins of the moneychangers and overturned their tables. And He said to those who sold the pigeons, "Take these things out of here, and stop making my Father's house a marketplace" (John 2:16). When Jesus said that, immediately, the disciples remembered Psalm 69:9, which said, "Zeal for Your house will consume me." Jesus was consumed by His zeal for God's house.

Jesus entered the temple that day looking for a place of prayer and found instead a marketplace. He went seeking communion with God and found the haggling of moneychangers. He went looking for sacrifice and found accountants and stockbrokers and money managers calculating the profits of the day. Here at the outset of His ministry, consumed by His zeal for God's house, Jesus exposed and challenged the corruption and abuse of religious power, and His anger became for Him the energy of righteousness.

So what are we to make of this story? And how does it apply to us on this? Well, for starters, this is as good a time as any for us to examine what makes us angry, how we express and deal with our anger, what our anger is really about, and what our anger says about us. This is a time for us to learn what we can from Jesus, who taught us how to be angry without sin.

I have to admit that sometimes I am afraid of people who get angry because many people do not know how to be angry without sin. They do not know how to channel their anger in productive ways. Rather than being the energy of righteousness, their anger becomes the catalyst for all kinds of destructive and self-destructive behavior. Rather than facing the truth about themselves, they take their anger out on other people. They never learn how to process their anger, but instead carry around unresolved bitterness and resentment about past injuries. They get angry about petty, unimportant issues that do not matter. They get angry and stay angry about the wrong things.

But I am even more afraid of what can happen to us when we do *not* become angry about the *right* things, when we lapse into a state of complacency, when we let things slide that are important to God, and even use our religion to settle for what Jesus courageously challenged. The only thing worse than misguided anger is no anger at all — no anger when we see the house of God turned into a clubhouse for members only, no anger when we see people using religion to advance their political agenda or to pad their pockets, no anger when church becomes a status symbol, no anger about the things that made Jesus angry. When anger is misguided, it is the energy for all kinds of destruction. But when anger is informed by Jesus, it is the energy of righteousness.

Anger can be our friend. It can energize us to do what is right. But it can also cause us to do what is wrong. That is why it is so important what is really going on inside us. And one question that might help us with this self-examination is this: Would Jesus be angry about this? If your anger is misguided, it will energize you to do what is wrong and hurtful and destructive. It will energize you to devalue others and exact vengeance to get even. But if your anger is informed by Jesus, if you care about what Jesus cares about, if you have passionate zeal for what Jesus is zealous about, then your anger will be what causes you to work for peace and justice, and your anger will become for you the energy of righteousness. Amen.

The Long-Awaited Kiss

An Advent Sermon

PSALM 85:1-2, 8-13

> ¹ *Lord, you were favorable to your land;*
> *you restored the fortunes of Jacob.*
> ² *You forgave the iniquity of your people;*
> *you pardoned all their sin. Selah*
> ³ *You withdrew all your wrath;*
> *you turned from your hot anger.*
>
> ⁴ *Restore us again, O God of our salvation,*
> *and put away your indignation toward us.*
> ⁵ *Will you be angry with us forever?*
> *Will you prolong your anger to all generations?*
> ⁶ *Will you not revive us again,*
> *so that your people may rejoice in you?*
> ⁷ *Show us your steadfast love, O Lord,*
> *and grant us your salvation.*
>
> ⁸ *Let me hear what God the Lord will speak,*
> *for he will speak peace to his people,*
> *to his faithful, to those who turn to him in their hearts.*
> ⁹ *Surely his salvation is at hand for those who fear him,*
> *that his glory may dwell in our land.*

> [10] *Steadfast love and faithfulness will meet;*
> *righteousness and peace will kiss each other.*
> [11] *Faithfulness will spring up from the ground,*
> *and righteousness will look down from the sky.*
> [12] *The Lord will give what is good,*
> *and our land will yield its increase.*
> [13] *Righteousness will go before him,*
> *and will make a path for his steps.*

A long time ago, movie and television directors figured out that there was one sure way to keep viewers engaged, and that was to develop a story line in which two characters are drawn to each other, but deny or resist their chemistry for one reason or another. Maybe there is a love triangle, or a barrier that separates them. Maybe their families or friends advise them against developing a romantic relationship. Maybe there is a love-hate relationship that makes a couple rotate between attraction and tension. Maybe it is a forbidden, but undeniable connection. But whatever it is, the writers develop the plot in such a way that viewers are as invested as the characters themselves. It seems as if it takes forever for the couple to give in to their undeniable feelings. The anticipation builds, and finally there is a long-awaited kiss. We all knew it needed to happen, and we all wondered if it ever would. If you are watching such a scene in a movie theater, sometimes applause spontaneously erupts when their lips finally meet.

Some of the younger people here might be thinking of some series on Netflix. Some of the senior adults might be thinking of the long-awaited kiss in *Gone with the Wind* between Clark Gable, as Rhett Butler, and Vivien Leigh, as Scarlett O'Hara in the 1939 epic. The more sophisticated among us might be thinking of the long-awaited kiss between Romeo and Juliet in Shakespeare's tragedy.

But when I think of a long-awaited kiss, I think of the TV show *Cheers* that ran from 1982 to 1993 in which Sam, played by Ted Danson, and Diane, played by Shelley Long, were the classic "will-they-or-won't-they" sitcom couple. They set the bar for long-awaited TV kiss, spending years annoying each other around the bar and ragging on one another — so much that we all knew it had to be true love. Then after a blow-out fight, they finally shared a kiss in the back office. Some of us thought it would never happen, and some of us knew it would eventually.

In Psalm 85, the psalmist uses poetic imagery to anticipate a time in the future when Steadfast Love and Faithfulness would be united, and Righteousness and Peace would finally, at long last, kiss each other. In verse 10, the poet is portraying the attributes of God, the virtues of God's nature, and the realities of God's character as if they were human figures. Using synonymous parallelism, the poet describes in the *first* part of verse 10 what he underscores in the *second* part of the verse. In the same verse, the poet makes a statement and then re-states in the next line the same thought using different words. So here in verse 10, we have two ways of affirming the same reality.

In the first pairing, two figures are moving in opposite directions — but rather than passing each other by, they meet. One is called Steadfast Love, the other is called Faithfulness. Depending on which translation you use, you might find that these two characters have different names. Steadfast Love is also called Mercy. And Faithfulness is also called Truth.

In the second pairing, two figures embrace or kiss each other. One is called Righteousness, the other Peace. A kiss was a common form of greeting in ancient times, and still is in some cultures. The word picture painted in verse 10 is one of two friends greeting each other as if they had been separated a long time. Righteousness and Peace had been estranged, but now they are friends again. They are reunited. And when they meet, there is a long-awaited kiss.

A man and wife were sitting in their living room when they noticed their neighbor across the street pull in to his driveway. He stepped out of the car with flowers in his hand, met his wife at the door, and laid a passionate kiss on her. As they watched all this play out across the street, the woman turned to her husband and wistfully said, "Why don't *you* do that?"

The man looked at his wife and replied, "Well, Honey, I hardly know the woman."

It is a sad, but true reality that we live in a world in which Truth and Mercy hardly know each other anymore. Righteousness and Peace are at odds with each other. They have been estranged for so long, and many of us have become so cynical that we have given up hope that they can ever meet again, let alone embrace and kiss. But the psalmist had not given up hope. The psalmist longed for the day when there could be a great reunion between Truth and Mercy, Righteousness and Peace.

Sometimes it seems as though these characters are at least opposites that do not attract, or even worse, enemies that fight against each other. But from the very beginning, these two attributes have been fully and completely united in the nature and character of God. *We* may see them as mutually exclusive. *We* may view them as opposites or enemies. But from cover to cover, the Bible sees these two characters blended into the nature and character of the one true God.

To be sure, in our lives, relationships, and politics, these two sets of virtues are estranged. Too many of us view ourselves as one way or the other. We see ourselves as either truthful and righteous, or merciful and peaceful. But never the two shall meet. Most of us err on one side or the other, or we make one the enemy of the other. Either we see the world through the lens of rules and principles or through the lens of relationships and people.

Righteousness and truth are those twin virtues that are concerned with doing what is *right*, whereas mercy and peace are those twin virtues that are concerned with doing what is *good*. Too many of us make what is *right* the *enemy* of what is *good*, and vice versa. Either we see the world in black-and-white categories, or we see everything in shades of gray. Righteousness and Peace are estranged within us — and because we cannot figure out a way to bring the two together, or because we are unwilling to do the hard and sacrificial work necessary for Righteousness and Peace to kiss rather than fight, we just dig in our heels and choose one over the other, never stopping to consider how incomplete one is without the other.

Righteousness without peace devolves into legalism. Peace without righteousness degenerates into permissiveness. Righteousness without peace is too hard, and peace without righteousness is too soft.

A concern for righteousness without a corresponding concern for peace invariably degenerates into self-righteousness — a callous, superior disregard for other people. All that matters is that I do what is right. The only problem with that approach, and it is a big problem, is that doing what is right also involves showing mercy and making peace.

But on the other hand, peacemaking without a moral compass becomes nothing more than a mushy sentimentality that stands for nothing and falls for anything. Showing mercy without advocating for what is right and true invariably turns into pandering, and giving up what is true in order to please people. All that matters is that I do what is good. The only problem with that approach, and it is a big problem, is that doing what is good also involves speaking the truth and doing what is right.

But imagine what would happen if those two qualities came together with a kiss. That's what the psalmist did. He let himself dream about a day when righteousness and peace would co-exist in perfect harmony and unity. I believe that, if there is anything wrong with our world today, it is that Truth and Mercy too seldom meet. Righteousness and Peace have become mutually exclusive. And two huge obstacles that stand in the way is an astounding lack of humility, and an alarming lack of self-awareness. Most of us are not even aware of the gaping holes in our own character.

It seemed to me that the world got a little darker when I heard that Clyde Wright had died. Clyde was the revered pastor of Brandon Baptist Church in Greenville, South Carolina, for almost thirty years. He was a mentor and a friend to many of us in my generation who were young enough to be his children in ministry. At a very difficult time in my life, just before I came to Earle Street, God brought our lives together. He encouraged me when I was discouraged and believed in me when I did not believe in myself. He was a spiritual giant to me — a marvelous example of a husband, father, grandfather, pastor, and friend. Clyde was what I would call a "gentle conservative," an extraordinary example of what happens in the life of a believer in whom Truth and Mercy meet, and Righteousness and Peace kiss each other. His quest for righteousness never diminished his passion for peace, and his passion for peace in no way diminished his quest for righteousness. Every now and then, if we are fortunate, God brings someone like that into our lives to show us what it looks like when righteousness and peace are no longer enemies or strangers, but friends.

The vast majority of us err on one side or the other. The people who know us best immediately recognize us as being too hard or too soft. But rarely, we run across people like Clyde Wright who are hard to peg. When asked if Clyde were too hard or too soft, the people who knew him best would have to think long and hard. Both biblical instincts were so obvious in him that it would be hard to say whether he was too hard or too soft. I want to be that kind of person because I have decided to follow Jesus, who fully embodied what the psalmist dreamed of.

From the beginning of Scripture, and throughout the Old Testament, God is described as being a God of both truth and mercy, righteousness and peace until, in the fullness of time, the very Word by which the world was spoken into existence, in the words of John, "became flesh and lived among us … full of both grace and truth" (John 1:14) — not half one and half the other, but fully both. The dream of the poet of Psalm 85 was fulfilled in the Person of Jesus, in whom Truth and Mercy met, and in whom Righteousness and Peace embraced and kissed. Mercy and Truth, Righteousness and Peace, greet each other in Jesus and in all of us who will follow Him. So we pray that the dream of the psalmist fulfilled in the life, death, and resurrection of Jesus would also be expressed in the lives of His followers as we work together, by the power of God, to create a world in which Righteousness and Peace come together in a warm embrace and a long-awaited kiss — perfect harmony and perfect unity. But it may be today that before we get to work to create that kind of world, God will need to do some work in us so that when someone we love is asked whether we are too hard or too soft, that person, rather than immediately blurting out the obvious answer, might need some time to think about it because the two virtues are so inextricably woven together that it is hard to tell where one starts and the other stops. So let there be peace on earth, but let there be righteousness, too. Amen.

The Path of Peace

LUKE 1:67-80

⁶⁷ *Then his father Zechariah was filled with the Holy Spirit and spoke this prophecy:*

⁶⁸ *"Blessed be the Lord God of Israel,*
for he has looked favorably on his people and redeemed them.
⁶⁹ *He has raised up a mighty savior for us*
in the house of his servant David,
⁷⁰ *as he spoke through the mouth of his holy prophets from of old,*
⁷¹ *that we would be saved from our enemies*
and from the hand of all who hate us.
⁷² *Thus he has shown the mercy promised to our ancestors,*
and has remembered his holy covenant,
⁷³ *the oath that he swore to our ancestor Abraham,*
to grant us ⁷⁴ *that we, being rescued from the hands of our enemies,*
might serve him without fear,
⁷⁵ *in holiness and righteousness before him all our days.*
⁷⁶ *And you, child, will be called the prophet of the Most High;*
for you will go before the Lord to prepare his ways,
⁷⁷ *to give knowledge of salvation to his people*
by the forgiveness of their sins.
⁷⁸ *By the tender mercy of our God,*
the dawn from on high will break upon [b] *us,*

[79] *to give light to those who sit in darkness and in the shadow of death,*
to guide our feet into the way of peace."

[80] *The child grew and became strong in spirit, and he was in the wilderness until the day he appeared publicly to Israel.*

Peace is not just a place to stand; it is a path in which to walk. It is not just a feeling; it is a way of life. It is not just the absence of conflict or anxiety; peace is the active presence and work of God. Peace is a path. **And like many paths, it is surrounded on both sides by ditches.** In fact, the ditches on both sides actually define the path between them. The way to *avoid* the ditches is to *identify* the ditches and stay on the path, and the way to stay on the path is to do what my brother Howell told me when he was teaching me to drive: Keep it between the ditches. Peace is not a place to stand; it is a path in which to walk.

I did not come up with this myself. These were among the first words spoken by Zechariah, the father of John the Baptizer, who had been unable to speak for nine months. It all started when the angel Gabriel announced that he and his wife, Elizabeth, would have a son named John. Zechariah was at best curious, if not skeptical, about how this could be, seeing as how both he and Elizabeth were "advanced in years," as he put it. It was a reasonable question, and I am quite sure that Zechariah would not have been the only one asking it. But Gabriel took a dim view of Zechariah's question, and told Zechariah that because he did not believe Gabriel, he would be unable to speak for nine whole months until his son was born. Can you imagine what it would be like not to be able to speak for nine whole months?

For Zechariah, that must have been miserable. After all, he was a priest. And what priest, or preacher, does not like to talk? And as for the people who were waiting outside the temple to receive words of blessing from Zechariah, they were in for a long wait. On the other hand, those nine months might have been easier for Elizabeth. After all, many pregnant mothers are more annoyed than comforted by their husbands' feeble attempts to make things easier with their words. Most husbands in cases like that would probably get into less trouble and would please their pregnant wives more by being silent for nine months. But in Zechariah's case, he had no choice. For nine months, if he wanted to communicate something to Elizabeth, he had to use sign language, play charades, or scribble his words on parchment.[26]

Another way to look at this situation is to consider the reality that not just priests, but expectant fathers, can learn so much more by listening than by talking. Zechariah had much to learn about preparing to be a first-time father in his old age. He had to learn about the changes going on in Elizabeth's body, not to mention her heart and soul, as the baby inside her developed and even leaped for joy in her womb. And, as a priest, Zechariah had to learn about the ways of God that he could have only learned through silence. Nine months of silence …

You have probably heard the story about the monk who had taken a vow of silence. And every ten years, this monk was allowed to break the vow of silence to speak only two words. After the first ten years, the monk had his first chance to speak two words. And he said, "Food bad." Ten years later, when he was allowed to speak two words, he said, "Bed hard." Then another decade passed. And when the time came for the monk to speak his two words, he gave the head monk a long stare and said, "I quit."

The head monk replied, "I'm not surprised, you've been complaining ever since you got here."

---

26 Barbara Brown Taylor. *Bread of Angels* (Cambridge, Massachusetts: Cowley Publications, 1997), 93.

Well, there are some obvious differences between Zechariah and this monk. The most obvious difference is that the monk's vow of silence was voluntary. Zechariah was involuntarily silent. But another difference which is important to notice is that, when his son was born, and Zechariah's tongue was loosed, the first words out of his mouth were words of blessing ("benedictus"), not complaint. Whatever inconvenience and frustration he experienced during his nine months of silence paled in comparison to the utter joy he experienced when his son was born.

Maybe it was because Zechariah for the first time in his life was not expected to speak, but was forced to listen. Maybe it was because, for nine months, he had been listening to his wife Elizabeth, and listening for the voice of God. But for whatever reason, when his son was born and his tongue was loosed, he was filled with the Holy Spirit and began to prophesy. I don't know this, and I certainly cannot prove it from the text, but I believe that these words of blessing were given to him not just in that moment, but had been given to him for the past nine months. By being forced to listen, his heart was filled with words of blessing: "Blessed be the Lord God of Israel," he said, "for he has looked favorably on his people and redeemed them. He has raised up a mighty savior for us" (Luke 1:68-69). His words were not just words of blessing; they were also words of prophecy. The Holy Spirit gave Zechariah a vision of the ministry God would give to his son, John. After his words of blessing to God, Zechariah offered words of prophecy to his newborn son: "And you, child, will be called the prophet of the Most High; for you will go before the Lord to prepare His ways, to give knowledge of salvation to His people by the forgiveness of their sins. By the tender mercy of our God … to guide our feet into the *path of peace*" (Luke 1:76-79).

Once Zechariah was able to speak, he spoke with such eloquent vision that no one could doubt the Source of those words. Just as God, through the angel Gabriel, silenced Zechariah for a time, now God at the birth of Zechariah's son, John, opened Zechariah's mouth and loosed his tongue to speak words of blessing and prophecy. Zechariah saw in the moment what we see now only in retrospect: that his son, John the Baptizer, would prepare the way for the birth of the Messiah, clearing out a path for his cousin Jesus, who would walk on that path Himself, and would guide our feet to walk on the same path. And according to Zechariah's prophetic words, this path was the path of peace. In this prophecy, Zechariah was able to envision, and give us a glimpse of, what Jesus more completely showed us: that peace is not a place to stand, but a path in which to walk.

And like many paths, the path of peace is surrounded on both sides by ditches, which give contour and definition to the path. **On one side is the ditch of unbridled aggression.** Some people think that the only way to achieve peace is to crush the enemy, to defeat the opposition with sheer force. One way to end conflict is to overpower your enemy. But the biblical notion of peace is not the mere absence of conflict. Just because there is no more open hostility does not mean there is peace. Peace is marked not by what is missing, but by what is present. It is the presence of wholeness and completeness, well-being and security. Aggression, hostility, retaliation, and violence are not the path of peace, but a ditch in which many people, even so-called Christ followers, get stuck. Jesus called us not to overpower our enemies, but to love them; not to use force against them, but to pray for them; not to retaliate, but to turn the other cheek. I know, I know that in this kind of world torn apart by violence and terrorism, the path of peace seems impractical and unworkable. But my job is not to solve the world's problems. My job as a pastor is to tell you what Jesus said and what Jesus did — and my job as a follower of Jesus is to follow Him on this path that Zechariah envisioned, that his son John cleared out, and that Jesus walked — because peace is not a place in which to stand, but a path in which to walk.

But there is another ditch on the other side of the path of peace. It is the ditch of passiveness. Some people believe that the only way to achieve peace is to avoid conflict altogether, to lie down and do nothing, to surrender and give up, to leave well enough alone, to let sleeping dogs lie, or to just let our enemies run all over us. That's another way to avoid conflict — just disengage, isolate, withdraw, give up and give in, and let your enemies win. But again, peace is not just the absence of conflict. It is almost impossible to trace this quotation back to its original source. It is often attributed to Edmund Burke, but regardless of who said it, it is true: "The only thing necessary for the triumph of evil is for good men to do nothing." Peace is not achieved by doing nothing. Jesus did not say, "Blessed are the peace*keepers*," but "blessed are the peace*makers*" (Matthew 5:9a). Peace is not a passive idea. In fact, it is not an idea at all. It is a path in which to walk. It is an active, risky way of life. Whatever else you want to say about Jesus, He was not passive. He challenged the status quo. He exposed evil and self-righteousness, and called it what it was. He made enemies by the way He lived. He never said that we should have no enemies. In fact, Jesus assumed that if we walk on the path of peace, and live as He lived, we would make enemies just as He did. So we can learn from Jesus not just how to win friends and influence people; we can also learn from Jesus how to make enemies and alienate people. There is a right way and a right reason for making enemies. When we make enemies, we should be sure we are making enemies in the same way and for the same reason Jesus did — not for the petty, self-righteous, self-serving reasons we tend to make enemies. If we make enemies, it should always be for the big reasons and the best reasons — justice and mercy, truth and love. And we do not have to stray off the path of peace to do justice, to show mercy, to speak truth, and to walk in love.

Zechariah envisioned it. His son, John the Baptist, cleared it out.

Their cousin Jesus walked it and called us to follow: it is the path of peace. You don't stand still on a path. You walk on it. And as we follow Jesus along this path of peace, we will avoid the ditches of aggression and passiveness on either side. Centuries before Zechariah uttered his prophecy, another prophet envisioned the coming Messiah and named Him, among other things, "the Prince of Peace." If we will follow the Prince of Peace along this path of peace, we will discover with great joy that this path will lead us all the way home, and we will discover that peace on earth, goodwill to all is more than just an angel's song. Amen.

Walking in the Light That Has Been Given to Us

JOHN 9:1-25

¹ As he walked along, he saw a man blind from birth. ² His disciples asked him, "Rabbi, who sinned, this man or his parents, that he was born blind?" ³ Jesus answered, "Neither this man nor his parents sinned; he was born blind so that God's works might be revealed in him. ⁴ We must work the works of him who sent me while it is day; night is coming when no one can work. ⁵ As long as I am in the world, I am the light of the world." ⁶ When he had said this, he spat on the ground and made mud with the saliva and spread the mud on the man's eyes, ⁷ saying to him, "Go, wash in the pool of Siloam" (which means Sent). Then he went and washed and came back able to see. ⁸ The neighbors and those who had seen him before as a beggar began to ask, "Is this not the man who used to sit and beg?" ⁹ Some were saying, "It is he." Others were saying, "No, but it is someone like him." He kept saying, "I am the man." ¹⁰ But they kept asking him, "Then how were your eyes opened?" ¹¹ He answered, "The man called Jesus made mud, spread it on my eyes, and said to me, 'Go to Siloam and wash.' Then I went and washed and received my sight." ¹² They said to him, "Where is he?" He said, "I do not know."

¹³ They brought to the Pharisees the man who had formerly been blind. ¹⁴ Now it was a sabbath day when Jesus made the

> mud and opened his eyes. ¹⁵ Then the Pharisees also began to ask him how he had received his sight. He said to them, "He put mud on my eyes. Then I washed, and now I see." ¹⁶ Some of the Pharisees said, "This man is not from God, for he does not observe the sabbath." But others said, "How can a man who is a sinner perform such signs?" And they were divided. ¹⁷ So they said again to the blind man, "What do you say about him? It was your eyes he opened." He said, "He is a prophet."
>
> ¹⁸ The Jews did not believe that he had been blind and had received his sight until they called the parents of the man who had received his sight ¹⁹ and asked them, "Is this your son, who you say was born blind? How then does he now see?" ²⁰ His parents answered, "We know that this is our son, and that he was born blind; ²¹ but we do not know how it is that now he sees, nor do we know who opened his eyes. Ask him; he is of age. He will speak for himself." ²² His parents said this because they were afraid of the Jews; for the Jews had already agreed that anyone who confessed Jesus to be the Messiah would be put out of the synagogue. ²³ Therefore his parents said, "He is of age; ask him."
>
> ²⁴ So for the second time they called the man who had been blind, and they said to him, "Give glory to God! We know that this man is a sinner." ²⁵ He answered, "I do not know whether he is a sinner. One thing I do know, that though I was blind, now I see."

If you have heard me preach for any length of time, the chances are good that you have heard me say this more than once. In fact, you may even be tired of hearing it. It is a statement that my former pastor, Ansel McGill, used to make every Sunday after the sermon as he gave the invitation to follow Jesus. It is the clearest way I know to invite people into a faith relationship with Jesus. "Give as much of yourself as you know how to as much of Jesus as you can understand."

Let's face it. None of us understands all there is to understand about Jesus. He is always beyond anything we can say, think, feel, imagine, or understand. But our relationship with Jesus is not based on our ability to understand Him. From *His* standpoint, it is based upon His grace alone. But from *our* standpoint, it is based on our willingness to trust Him.

In my kind of work, it is not unusual at all for me to get into conversations with people about how we can put our faith in anyone we cannot see or understand. Sometimes the question comes from an *insider*, one who has been in the church his or her whole life. "How do we know that what we have been taught about Jesus is true?" Sometimes the same question comes from someone *outside* the church who does not believe in Jesus because the Christian faith seems so irrational. Why *do* we believe in Jesus? How *do* we know that Jesus is real? Well, those of us who have been reared in the church might be inclined to say too quickly, "Because the Bible says so." But of course, that answer does not even satisfy everyone *in* the church, let alone those *outside* the faith. If you say you believe Jesus is real because the Bible tells you so, then it won't take long for a thinking person to reply: "Well, how do you know the Bible is reliable?" It is a good question, and one that we should be prepared to answer. But if you have ever gotten into this kind of philosophical or theological debate with someone, you know that you can only answer so many "how-do-you-know?" questions before you find yourself saying, "I don't know. I just know," which is about what the healed man said in this passage of Scripture from John's Gospel.

Upon leaving the temple one Sabbath day, Jesus saw a man who had been blind from birth, and who apparently was accustomed to begging outside the temple gate. Stating that He was "the light of the world," Jesus spat on the ground, made clay of the spittle, and anointed the man's eyes with the clay, saying to him, "Go, wash in the pool of Siloam"

(John 9:7). So the blind man did as he was told. He went and washed and came back seeing.

It all began in the heart of Jesus, who found this blind man long before the blind man found Him, who saw the blind man long before the blind man could see Him (or anyone else, for that matter). After anointing the man's eyes with spittle (which was a common method and custom of that time), Jesus sent him to wash in the pool of Siloam, which was apparently a test of the blind beggar's faith and obedience. So the amazing grace of Jesus, coupled with the faithful obedience of the blind man, resulted in a cure. John tells us that after the blind man did as He was instructed by Jesus, he came back seeing. It was a remarkable experience by anyone's standards — and like any extraordinary experience like that, it aroused the attention and the questions of cynics and skeptics who would not believe it if they could not understand it.

John tells us that soon the neighbors and those who had seen the blind man before as a beggar began questioning him about his healing. After he told them about his experience, they took him to the Pharisees who also questioned him about his healing. So the man repeated his account of the healing for the Pharisees, who immediately concluded that Jesus could not possibly be from God or He would not have violated the Sabbath laws, which, according to them, He had violated in two ways. First, He had acted on the Sabbath when no emergency endangered human life. And second, in mixing the dust with His spittle to make clay, Jesus was guilty of doing a kind of work that was forbidden on the day of rest. Then there were other Pharisees who argued quite the opposite: that anyone who was *not* from God could not have performed such a sign as the healing of a blind man. Consequently, there was division among the Pharisees. So at that point, the Pharisees pressured the healed man to assign some meaning to his experience — and about the best explanation that the healed man could come up with was that whoever healed him must have been a prophet.

Not content with that explanation, the Jews called in the healed man's parents to verify that, in fact, he had really been blind from birth, and to see to whom his *parents* would attribute the healing. They confirmed that the man indeed had been blind ever since his birth but they would neither confirm nor deny their son's testimony regarding his healing. "Ask him," they said. "He is of age. He will speak for himself" (John 9:21). Now John tells us that they said this because they feared the Jews and were afraid of being put out of the synagogue.

So for the second time, they called the healed man and asked him if his Healer was a sinner. Sensing that their question was a trick question, the healed man had the good sense to simply fall back on his experience. He didn't know the theology of what had happened. He didn't even know for sure who Jesus was, let alone whether He was a sinner or not. All he knew was that Jesus had transformed his life. "I do not know whether he is a sinner. One thing I *do* know, that though I was blind, now I see" (John 9:25).

Again, the Pharisees began debating this man. They could not argue with his *experience*, so they started questioning his *theology*. They would not *accept* it if they could not *explain* it in their own terms. If it did not fit into their theological system about how God works, they would dismiss the whole experience as invalid: "We know that God does not listen to sinners" (John 9:31), they said. "We have God figured out. We know how God works. And if your experience of God does not match our understanding of God, then your experience must not be valid" (my paraphrase). So they cast him out. They discounted his experience, and they dismissed him as being uninformed or unorthodox.

But when Jesus heard that they had cast out this man whom He had healed, again Jesus took the initiative to seek him out and tell him who

He was. The blind man said, "Lord, I believe" (John 9:38), and with that confession of faith, he worshiped Jesus. First, Jesus was a stranger to this man, then a prophet, and ultimately the object of his worship. As he walked in the light that Jesus had given him, he grew in his understanding of who Jesus was — the light of the world.

An ounce of personal experience is worth a pound of theory. Most of us find it difficult to make a theological argument about Jesus that will confound the theologians, silence the critics, satisfy the cynics, and convince the skeptics. All we can do is what this healed man did — just share our experience with Jesus and tell people what He means to us, and what He has done for us that we could not do for ourselves. All we can do is tell our truth and share our experience — and then live a life that is consistent with the experience we claim we have had.

So how will you know that you have had an experience with Jesus? I don't know. You'll just know. You may not be able to describe it or explain it, but you will be so transformed by it that no one will be able to persuade you otherwise. And if anyone ever asks you who Jesus is, maybe you could start by saying something like what this healed man said: "I don't know how to explain it fully. I just know that once was blind, but now I can see."

Every year, our church participates in one-day community missions blitz called "Operation Inasmuch," in which we have an opportunity to be the hands and feet of Jesus, to show His amazing grace, to shine His light to the people around us. And we can only hope that some of the people we serve might be able to say something like what this healed man said: "I do not know who sent these people to help me. I do not know why they would give up a Saturday to love someone they do not even know. All I know is that I was hungry, and they gave me something to eat. I was homeless, and they helped me. I was lonely, and they talked to me. I was desperate, and they brought some beauty into my life. I was hopeless, and they restored my hope that someone cares. They must be for real. And whoever sent them to me must be special." On that day every year, we look for opportunities to tell the people we serve that Jesus is the One who sent us, and that they can know Him truly without knowing Him fully. We just invite people to just give as much of themselves as they know how to as much of Jesus as they can understand. That's what *we* did. That's what *we* still do. Every day, we grow in our understanding of Jesus as we follow Him and walk in the light that He gives us.

We believe that Jesus is the light of the world, and that in Him, there is no darkness at all. Moreover, we believe that we are not supposed to hide the light under a bushel, but shine His light to the world around us. We may not understand all there is to know about Jesus. We may not be able to answer all the questions. But if we will just walk in whatever measure of light we have been given, if we will just give as much of ourselves as we know how to as much of Jesus as we can understand, if we will just shine His light to the world around us, we might be surprised at how much brighter our lives and our world will become. If we will just step in the light, walk in the light, and shine the light of Jesus, that light will lead us all the way home. Amen.

Walking the Fine Line

MICAH 6:1-8

¹ *Hear what the Lord says:*
Rise, plead your case before the mountains,
and let the hills hear your voice.
² *Hear, you mountains, the controversy of the Lord,*
and you enduring foundations of the earth;
for the Lord has a controversy with his people,
and he will contend with Israel.

³ *"O my people, what have I done to you?*
In what have I wearied you? Answer me!
⁴ *For I brought you up from the land of Egypt,*
and redeemed you from the house of slavery;
and I sent before you Moses,
Aaron, and Miriam.
⁵ *O my people, remember now what King Balak of Moab devised,*
what Balaam son of Beor answered him,
and what happened from Shittim to Gilgal,
that you may know the saving acts of the Lord."

⁶ *"With what shall I come before the Lord,*
and bow myself before God on high?
Shall I come before him with burnt offerings,
with calves a year old?

> ⁷ *Will the Lord be pleased with thousands of rams,*
> *with ten thousands of rivers of oil?*
> *Shall I give my firstborn for my transgression,*
> *the fruit of my body for the sin of my soul?"*
> ⁸ *He has told you, O mortal, what is good;*
> *and what does the Lord require of you*
> *but to do justice, and to love kindness,*
> *and to walk humbly with your God?*

Several years ago, some of the children in our church interviewed me. Some of their questions were easy to answer, like, "What is your favorite food?" Some of their questions were somewhat disturbing, like, "Do you have a real job?" and "What do you do the rest of the week?" But the question that got my attention most was, "What is the biggest challenge of being a pastor?" I did not even have to think about that one. The biggest challenge of being a pastor is trying to please God and please everybody else in the church. In that sense, this job is impossible. It's definitely not as easy as it looks, but it is probably not any harder than your job either. We all are caught in the tension of trying to please God and also please people. And sometimes I wonder which is harder.

In the eighth century before Christ, the covenant people were enjoying a time of economic prosperity, and many of them assumed that their affluence was a sign of God's favor and blessing upon them. It is a trap that is easy for religious people to fall into. I catch myself falling into that same kind of mentality when the budget offerings of our church exceed our budget requirements. Surely our surplus must be a sign that God is pleased with us. But in the midst of peace and prosperity, the Lord sent prophets like Amos, Hosea, Isaiah, and Micah to the people of God to proclaim a message that nobody wanted to hear. God was not as pleased with them as they were with themselves. And in the passage we read from the prophecy of Micah, God's word becomes crystal clear. The LORD had a controversy with the people of Judah because they had been lulled into a state of forgetfulness. They had forgotten what it was like to be poor slaves in a foreign land. Centuries removed from their people's bondage, they had forgotten what God had done for them, how God had redeemed them from slavery in Egypt, led them to the land of promise, sustained and protected them for centuries. But through the years, somehow they had grown indifferent to the needs of those around them. All of a sudden, they were the ones in a position of power, and they became defensive when they heard the scathing word of the LORD through the prophet Micah.

After all, they were still performing their religious duties on cue. They were still participating in all the religious rituals that gave them a false sense of security. What was it going to take to please God? What more did God want from them? Burnt offerings with calves a year old? Would the LORD be pleased if they offered thousands of rams, or ten thousand rivers of oil? What were they going to have to do to please God — give up their first-born children to atone for their sins?

In our religious culture, we might ask ourselves the same kinds of questions. What is it going to take to please God? How often do I have to come to church? Do I have to give a tithe of my income or more than a tithe? How much does God want? Do I have to participate in communion, come to this meeting and that meeting, be in church every Sunday and Wednesday? How many committees do I have to serve on? Do I have to spend hours every day in prayer and Bible reading? Am I going to have to be a missionary to Africa? What is it going to take to please God?

"Whoa," Micah says. "You can't please God by just practicing religion. God is not impressed with your religious busy-ness. You are making your covenant with God too complicated. God has shown you what is good. The requirements to please God are the following: to do justice, to love mercy, and to walk humbly.

To do justice, or to act justly, is to concern ourselves with what is right. It is to have a reliable moral compass. It is to act consistently with the righteous and holy character of God. It is to enforce and apply the law of God, both its letter and its spirit. It is to take God at God's word. It is to live with the belief that God means what God says and God says what God means. It is to be concerned with moral absolutes. It is to draw clear lines between what is right and what is wrong. It is to set high moral standards. It is to look around at the injustices around us and how we may be actually perpetuating the very injustices we say we deplore. Walter Brueggemann said that to do justice is to "sort out what belongs to whom, and to return it to them."[27] It is to redescribe the world as God sees it. It is to do what is right.

And let's be honest, if the list of God's requirements were to stop there, some of us would be very happy. But it doesn't. We long for a world in which right is still right and wrong is still wrong. We want people to do right and to be punished when they do not. We want people to earn their own way and get what they deserve. We want life to be fair and people to do right. But when concern for that kind of justice is all there is, inevitably we fall into the traps of self-righteousness, legalism, and selectivity. When we try to convince ourselves and others that all God wants is what is right, then we begin to assume that we know better than others what is right. We draw lines that keep us in and others out. We reduce the life of faith to a set of rules and laws, and we get very selective about what rules are important.

But Micah reminds us that God's covenant with us is not just about

---

27 Walter Brueggemann, "Voices of the Night — Against Justice," *To Act Justly, Love Tenderly, Walk Humbly: an Agenda for Ministers* (New York: Paulist Press, 1986), 5.

doing what is *right*. It is also about doing what is *good*. "He has shown you what is *good*" (Micah 6:8), Micah said. And it is not only to do justice, but it is also to love kindness. The Hebrew word translated "kindness" or "mercy" is a difficult word to capture in a single English word. Almost every translation of the Bible uses a different word or phrase to try to capture the essence of this rich Hebrew word. It is loving kindness, steadfast love, covenant love, loyal love. And it is every bit as much a part of God's nature as justice. God is as concerned with what is good as God is concerned with what is right. Even though God is righteous, God makes allowances for human sinfulness. Even though there is right and there is wrong, God restores and redeems and forgives those who do not and cannot live up to God's righteous standards. And here in this passage, Micah calls the people of God to temper their concern for justice with a love of mercy. Mercy is that instinct to move beyond fairness. It is to give people not what they deserve, but more than they deserve and better than they deserve. It is that faithful kind of love that stubbornly refuses to give up on people who miss the mark and fail to live up to the standards that have been set for them. It is to extend an open hand and an open heart to those who are broken and fallen. It is to make room for people who sin. It is to do unto others as we would have them do unto us. It is to show the mercy to others that God has shown to us.

But let's be honest about this requirement, too. When taken to an extreme and not tempered by a concern for what is right, the instinct to be kind and merciful can degenerate into permissiveness. God becomes some kind of sugar daddy who kind of winks at sin, but doesn't take it seriously. Those who love kindness without doing justice can adopt an "anything-goes" mentality. They help to create an atmosphere that does not set high standards. They turn commandments into suggestions, and find a way to explain or even excuse unacceptable behavior.

And let's face it, we all find ourselves somewhere on the continuum between justice and kindness, between judgment and mercy. All of us tend to live our lives leaning in one of these directions or the other. But that is why there is a third requirement that keeps the first two together in a healthy tension. God has shown us what is good and what is required: to do justice, to love kindness, and to walk humbly with our God.

If there is any quality that is missing in our culture, in our national debates, in our churches, in our denomination, and in our families, it is humility. When you think about it, humility is the only way we *can* walk with God. Those who concern themselves primarily with justice and those who concern themselves primarily with mercy are all in danger of becoming blind to the truth that we do not and cannot see the world as God sees it. We do not have all the truth. We cannot know all that we need to know. We may be right, but we are never completely right. We may be good, but we are never completely good. That is why this third requirement is so crucial. When we reach the end of our capacities, there is always more than what we can see. There is usually some measure of truth on the other side of the argument. But only those who walk humbly with God will even be willing to look for it. Only those who walk humbly with God are willing to say, "This is what I believe," but I could be wrong. Only those who walk humbly with God are open to new truth and new direction and new ways of living.

Micah was right — but hundreds of years before the coming of Jesus, he could not have known how right he was. In Jesus Christ, God *has* shown us what is good and what the Lord requires of us. In His life and ministry, Jesus showed us what it means to do justice, to love mercy, and to walk humbly with God. And until we balance justice and mercy with humility like He did, we still have some growing to do.

I have about decided that it is easier to please God than it is to please people. And the older I live, the more convinced I am that it is the *desire* to please God that pleases God. As a pastor, I am slowly realizing that I am never going to be able to please all of you, as much as I want to. I am going to have my hands full just trying to please God, which is as simple and as complicated as balancing justice and mercy with humility. That is what God requires of all of us. And in the life and ministry of Jesus Christ, God has shown us how it is done. Amen.

Why the Cover-up Is Worse Than the Crime

2 SAMUEL 11:1-15

¹ *In the spring of the year, the time when kings go out to battle, David sent Joab with his officers and all Israel with him; they ravaged the Ammonites, and besieged Rabbah. But David remained at Jerusalem.*

² *It happened, late one afternoon, when David rose from his couch and was walking about on the roof of the king's house, that he saw from the roof a woman bathing; the woman was very beautiful.* ³ *David sent someone to inquire about the woman. It was reported, "This is Bathsheba daughter of Eliam, the wife of Uriah the Hittite."* ⁴ *So David sent messengers to get her, and she came to him, and he lay with her. (Now she was purifying herself after her period.) Then she returned to her house.* ⁵ *The woman conceived; and she sent and told David, "I am pregnant."*

⁶ *So David sent word to Joab, "Send me Uriah the Hittite." And Joab sent Uriah to David.* ⁷ *When Uriah came to him, David asked how Joab and the people fared, and how the war was going.* ⁸ *Then David said to Uriah, "Go down to your house, and wash your feet." Uriah went out of the king's house, and there followed him a present from the king.* ⁹ *But Uriah slept at the entrance of the king's house with all the servants of his lord, and did not go down to his house.* ¹⁰ *When they told David, "Uriah did not go down*

to his house," David said to Uriah, "You have just come from a journey. Why did you not go down to your house?" ¹¹ *Uriah said to David, "The ark and Israel and Judah remain in booths; and my lord Joab and the servants of my lord are camping in the open field; shall I then go to my house, to eat and to drink, and to lie with my wife? As you live, and as your soul lives, I will not do such a thing."* ¹² *Then David said to Uriah, "Remain here today also, and tomorrow I will send you back." So Uriah remained in Jerusalem that day. On the next day,* ¹³ *David invited him to eat and drink in his presence and made him drunk; and in the evening he went out to lie on his couch with the servants of his lord, but he did not go down to his house.*

¹⁴ *In the morning David wrote a letter to Joab, and sent it by the hand of Uriah.* ¹⁵ *In the letter he wrote, "Set Uriah in the forefront of the hardest fighting, and then draw back from him, so that he may be struck down and die."*

"The cover-up is worse than the crime." How many times have you heard that line? The first time I remember hearing this phrase was when I was a teenager during the Watergate scandal. But I have heard it many times since then, even recently, applied to politicians of both parties. I guess it depends on what the crime is whether the cover-up is worse. But then again, the reason the cover-up is worse than the crime is that the cover-up compounds the crime.

After reading the passage of Scripture, instead of saying "This is the Word of the Lord," I feel like I should be saying, "These are the days of our lives," or maybe, "These are the young and the restless" (or "the young and the reckless," as my father used to say). But this *is* the Word of the Lord. What makes the Bible so believable is that it does not idealize the people of God, even the heroes of our faith. The Bible makes it clear from the very beginning that all God has to work with are flawed human beings. The fact that God uses us at all is a tribute to God's grace. And the fact that David occupied such a prominent place in the story of God's people tells us more about the character of God than the character of David. This story is the Word of the Lord, but it still has all the makings of a successful Netflix series. There is lust and adultery, resulting in an untimely pregnancy, questions about the father of the child, deception and corruption at the highest levels of government, conspiracy, war and eventually death. Sin is sin and it is serious in and of itself — and often what makes sin even worse is the cover-up.

Sin can be likened to a pebble, and the cover-up can be likened to a pebble that is dropped in the water, creating a ripple effect. One sin, unconfessed and covered up, leads to another. One bad choice leads to another bad choice worse than the first.

I have used this illustration before. As you know, I have always been extremely bright. In fact, even as a child, I showed signs of being something of a prodigy. One day, I was playing in the dining room, which already gives you a clue as to just how smart I was. I threw a ball, never mind the fact that there was no one else in the room to catch it, and I broke a piece of our fine china. Because I was so bright, I knew that my mother would take a dim view of that incident — and if my father found out, he would speak those dreaded words that would put the fear of God in me: "You better give your heart to Jesus, because the rest is mine." So I knew I better act fast to cover up the damage done. So I found the super glue and tried to glue the broken pieces back together. But I accidentally got a glob of glue on the nicely varnished dining room table. But again, I was bright enough to know that I needed to wipe it off quickly before it dried. So I got a cotton ball to wipe off the glue, and the cotton stuck to the glue on the nicely varnished tabletop. But again, my intelligence paid off. I remembered hearing somewhere that nail polish remover would neutralize the stickiness of the glue. So I doused the glue spot with it, only to find out that nail polish remover does not actually remove *glue*, but it works wonders on removing *varnish*. Well, I won't bore you with the details of what happened after that. I will just tell you that I did give my heart to Jesus one more time, and my dad did get the rest. These kinds of stories can be entertaining when they involve things like super glue, nail polish remover, and varnish (although I must admit it was not all that entertaining to me at the time). But stories that involve the real lives and destinies of human beings are infinitely more serious and tragic.

When we pick up the story in this text, readers' discretion is advised. It is when life is going well that we are the most vulnerable. Up to this point, David had lived a charmed life. But we are never weaker than when we think we are strong. We are never more susceptible to danger than when we think we are safe. As the writer of Proverbs put it, "Pride goes before destruction" (Proverbs 16:18). And as Paul wrote to the Corinthians, "If you think you are standing, watch out that you do not fall" (1 Corinthians 10:12). David was not prepared for what was about to happen to him.

First of all, he was not where he was supposed to be. And already, there is a lesson to be learned as early as verse 1 of our text. It was the spring of the year, the time when kings are *supposed* to go out to battle along with the troops. But David sent *Joab*, his general, along with Joab's officers and troops, into battle while *he* stayed at home. Apparently, by this time in the narrative, David had reached a point at which he rose above the battle. He was much too powerful and important to put himself in harm's way, so he remained in Jerusalem. And we are left to wonder how this story would have turned out if David had been where he was supposed to be.

How much needless pain we inflict upon ourselves and others just because we are not where we are supposed to be. Do you ever find yourself in that kind of place and position? You look around and you know in your heart that is somewhere you should not be, and before you know what happened, you are doing something you should not do. This happens to me all the time when I am on a diet. Somehow I find myself at Krispy Kreme or Taco Bell or the Clock. When I am somewhere I should not be, it is so easy to do something I should not do. And that seems harmless enough when we are talking about gaining a few pounds — but when people's lives are at stake, it gets real serious real fast. We are, by nature, prone to wander, prone to leave the very God we love,[28] prone to be where we should not be. And if we will listen closely, when we are in those places, we might be able to hear the sound of a pebble as it splashes in the water.

David might not have originally intended to do something wrong. But he was in the wrong place at the wrong time. It was late one afternoon. David was home relaxing, perhaps minding his own business, maybe admiring the vastness of his kingdom, and feeling good about his accomplishments. He had made it big, and he was on his roof, basking not just in the warmth of the spring sun, but also in the success of his life — when he casually glanced from his rooftop and saw a beautiful woman bathing. And the rest is history.

David used his position of power to summons Bathsheba to his bedroom chamber. She was a woman in a world of men's voices and men's power. The text does not even allow us to hear her voice, except in her three-word message to King David, "I am pregnant." As a woman caught in the power politics and desires of a king, it is not as if she had much

---

28 Robert Robinson. *Come, Thou Fount of Every Blessing*. Public domain.

choice when the king sent for her. David always got what he wanted. At any rate, there is a very important detail in this story. Both David and Bathsheba were married to other people. David was married to several other people. He had many wives and concubines. But Bathsheba had a husband, whose name was Uriah. And Uriah was a loyal soldier, ironically fighting David's battles, while David was taking Uriah's wife.

What started out as a private glance from a rooftop continued as an adulterous affair. David sent for Bathsheba. In fact, forms of the verb "to send" are used nine times in this passage — and each time, except in verse 5, the sending is being done by David or at his will. Clearly, David had the power to send for people and move them around like pawns on a chess board. The moment David sent for Bathsheba, his servants were involved, obviously Bathsheba was involved, and Uriah was unwittingly involved. Sin's ripple effects have a way of taking us down and others with us. Our sinful choices have the potential to destroy not just us, but also the people around us. David might have thought he was not hurting anyone and that no one else would find out. But after a while, pregnancy is a little hard to hide. And as soon as the cover-up began, the ripples just kept multiplying and spreading out.

David's cover-up plan involved sending for Uriah and getting him home from battle so he could be with his wife and be deceived into thinking he was the father of Bathsheba's child. So again David sent for the unknowing, blindly loyal husband, just as he had sent for his wife earlier. And it would have been a perfect cover-up if Uriah had just cooperated. But he did not. Wouldn't you know that, out of all the women in Israel with whom David could have had an affair, he had to pick the one who had a husband of integrity? Uriah refused David's offer because he did not think it was fair for him to have the pleasure of being with his wife when the other soldiers were on the battlefield. So the cover-up continued. David got Uriah drunk, hoping that then

Uriah would stumble into his wife's arms, forgetting his honor and integrity. But even intoxication could not coax Uriah away from his high standards. David, now desperate, ordered Uriah back to the battlefield, and then ordered Joab, his general, to put Uriah on the front lines of battle and then pull back the rest of the troops so that Uriah could be killed in battle. And the cover-up continued. The ripple effects did not stop there. This situation started when David made the decision not to be where he was supposed to be, which led to lust, which led to adultery, which led to deception and conspiracy, and eventually the death of a good person.

My former pastor, Ansel McGill, used to make this statement rather frequently: "We are judged not so much *for* our sins, but *by* our sins." And the longer I live and minister, the more convinced I am of the truth of that statement. That is just another way of saying that sin carries with it its own set of consequences. And the consequences of our sins are multiplied when we try to cover them up, rather than confessing them and repenting of them in a timely way. Sometimes, according to the Bible, our own sins judge us. And the tragedy is not just that *we* are judged by our sins, but often *other people* are victimized by our sins as well.

The cover-up is worse than the crime because the cover-up always compounds the crime and leads to other sins. But the good news of the gospel is that the grace of God can cover up infinitely more than our worst sins and our most elaborate cover-up schemes. When David finally stopped trying to cover up his sins and instead confessed his sins to the Lord, he found out that he could not out-sin the grace of God. And neither can we. The Scripture teaches us that, when we confess our sins, God is faithful and just to forgive our sins and cleanse us of all unrighteousness (1 John 1:9). In other words, as horrible as our sin is, God's grace is greater. The cover-up never really "covers up" the sin; it only compounds it. We are sinners saved by grace. The sin is our own, but the grace is a gift from God. The only reality that can "cover up" the sin is the marvelous, infinite, matchless grace of God. Amen.

Why We Love the Lord

DEUTERONOMY 6:4-5; PSALM 18:1-2;
1 JOHN 4:13-19

---

⁴ Hear, O Israel: The Lord is our God, the Lord alone. ⁵ You shall love the Lord your God with all your heart, and with all your soul, and with all your might. — Deuteronomy 6:4-5

¹ I love you, O Lord, my strength.
² The Lord is my rock, my fortress, and my deliverer,
my God, my rock in whom I take refuge,
my shield, and the horn of my salvation, my stronghold.
— Psalm 18:1-2

¹³ By this we know that we abide in him and he in us, because he has given us of his Spirit. ¹⁴ And we have seen and do testify that the Father has sent his Son as the Savior of the world. ¹⁵ God abides in those who confess that Jesus is the Son of God, and they abide in God. ¹⁶ So we have known and believe the love that God has for us. God is love, and those who abide in love abide in God, and God abides in them. ¹⁷ Love has been perfected among us in this: that we may have boldness on the day of judgment, because as he is, so are we in this world. ¹⁸ There is no fear in love, but perfect love casts out fear; for fear has to do with punishment, and whoever fears has not reached perfection in love. ¹⁹ We love because he first loved us. — 1 John 4:13-19

When it gets right down to it, it is hard to say why we love the people we love. Why do you love your parents, your spouse, your friends? Sometimes when I am talking with married couples or couples who are about to be married, the question will come up: "Why do you love each other?" And it is not uncommon for there to be an awkward period of silence. Sometimes the silence is because the question caught them off guard. And sometimes the silence comes because the answer is hard to put into words. Sometimes the silence is there because we have never really thought about why. Love just comes so naturally for some people and takes on a life of its own. And no one really knows why. It just happens. Sometimes there is silence because there are so many reasons that it is hard to know where to begin. Why do I love thee? Let me count the reasons.

Well, the same principles apply when we talk about our love relationship with God. In fact, the Bible often compares God's love for us and our love for God in terms of a marital relationship. Of course, the analogy breaks down at a certain point, but that kind of human relationship helps us understand some of the dynamics of our relationships with God. Our love for God not just a private, internal love, but a missional kind of love that compels us not just to keep it, but to share it. It is not to be some kind of casual, half-hearted love, but an all-consuming kind of love that involves all that we have and all that we are — heart, soul, and strength — the primary love of our lives. What Jesus called the greatest commandment of all can be found in Deuteronomy 6:4-5. The fact that Jesus picked out a single commandment from all the 613 commandments in the Hebrew Scripture shows us how important and basic our love for God must be.

Those of us who have been conditioned to think of love as a *feeling* react against love as a *commandment*. How do you make yourself love someone — especially if love is a feeling? But that's just it. In the Western world, we tend to think of love primarily as a feeling. But in the Hebrew mindset, love was not primarily an emotion at all. That is why this kind of love could be commanded. Love is primarily an action to take, a promise to fulfill, a covenant to keep when we feel like it, and even when we do not. So the first reason we love God is that we have been commanded to. We are expected to. We are obligated to. We are supposed to.

Now, if you try to use those reasons in the context of a marriage relationship (or any other relationship, for that matter), they might not go over too well. So when the question is asked, "Why do you love me?" and your answer is, "because I have to," or "because I am supposed to," or "because I am obligated to," the other person might take a dim view of that answer. What kind of answer is that? I love you because I have been commanded to, because I have to?

But this passage is one of the many places in which the Bible is at odds with our culture. Doing something, especially loving someone, out of a sense of obligation can be a very noble reason. In fact, sometimes the highest, noblest reason for doing what we do is because we *have* to. Some of the most important things we do in life are things that we would not have chosen to do on our own, things we do not feel like doing, but things we were created and commanded to do. The first reason we love God, and maybe even the best reason, the highest, noblest reason for loving God is that we have been commanded to love God with all that we have and all that we are.

But that is certainly not the only reason we love God. The psalmist of Psalm 18 gives us another reason. We love God not just because we have to, but because of who God is and what God does. This psalm, also found in Second Samuel 22, is attributed to David, who addressed this song to the Lord on the day when the Lord delivered him from his enemies, and especially from Saul's threats. First, David said that he loved the Lord because of who God was to him: "The Lord is my rock and my fortress, my deliverer, my God, my shield, the horn of my salvation, my stronghold." In other words, the Lord can be trusted to shield us and protect us and save us from our enemies — because that is who God is.

Now I know that it does not always work out that way for us immediately. In fact, it did not always work out that way for David either, at least not immediately. Sometimes the Lord does not save us from our enemies in the short-run. Sometimes our enemies win. Sometimes the Lord does not shield and protect us from threats and dangers. Sometimes the Lord does not deliver us when and how we prefer and expect. But in those times when life is hard, we love the Lord anyway, trusting in God's ultimate purposes and plans for us that we cannot possibly see or understand. Sometimes the Lord delivers us from our immediate crises and gives us victory over our enemies. And sometimes, for God's own reasons, the Lord delays and disguises the victory. But even then, we still love God because of who God is.

In her song, *Trust in You*, Lauren Daigle wrote:

> *When You don't move the mountains I'm needing You to move*
> *When You don't part the waters I wish I could walk through*
> *When You don't give the answers as I cry out to You*
> *I will trust, I will trust, I will trust in You!*[29]

We love God because God can be trusted. We love God not just because we are commanded to, but because of who God is and what God does. We love God because God is great and God is good.

And of course, we love God because God first loved us. While we

---

29 Lauren Daigle. *Trust in You.* Copyright © 2014 CentricSongs (SESAC) See You At The Pub (SESAC) (adm. at CapitolCMGPublishing.com) All rights reserved. Used by permission.

were yet sinners, before we ever even knew God, God loved us first — even and especially when we did not deserve God's love, even when we do not return God's love, even when we turn our backs on God's love. There is nothing we could ever do to make God love us more or less than God already loves us. So we love God because we are loved *by* God. And some of us find that love hard to believe because of the way we feel about ourselves. But again, God's love for us is not based on feelings. It is based on a reality that is so intrinsic to God's nature that it cannot be described in terms of feelings or even actions. It is who God is. John wrote, "God is love, and those who abide in love abide in God, and God abides in them" (1 John 4:16). We are talking here not just about some character trait of God. We are talking about the essence of who God is. And if we ever love God at all, it will be because God loved us first.

So why do we love God? Because we have been commanded to, because of who God is and what God does, and because God loved us first. Love is who God is and what God does. And nowhere do we see a more compelling picture of that love than on the cross where Jesus stretched out His arms, as if to embrace the whole world, and died. While we were yet sinners, and even *because* we were sinners, "God so loved the world that He gave His only Son, so that everyone who believes in Him may not perish, but may have eternal life" (John 3:16). How can we do anything in return except love our God? It is the reason we were created. It is our highest call. It is the greatest commandment because love is not just what God does; it is who God is. And as God's children, love is to be what we do, and who we are, too. Amen.

You Are Here, But So Is God
JOSHUA 1:1-5; HEBREWS 13:1-6

¹ After the death of Moses the servant of the Lord, the Lord spoke to Joshua son of Nun, Moses' assistant, saying, ² "My servant Moses is dead. Now proceed to cross the Jordan, you and all this people, into the land that I am giving to them, to the Israelites. ³ Every place that the sole of your foot will tread upon I have given to you, as I promised to Moses. ⁴ From the wilderness and the Lebanon as far as the great river, the river Euphrates, all the land of the Hittites, to the Great Sea in the west shall be your territory. ⁵ No one shall be able to stand against you all the days of your life. As I was with Moses, so I will be with you; I will not fail you or forsake you. — Joshua 1:1-5

¹ Let mutual love continue. ² Do not neglect to show hospitality to strangers, for by doing that some have entertained angels without knowing it. ³ Remember those who are in prison, as though you were in prison with them; those who are being tortured, as though you yourselves were being tortured. ⁴ Let marriage be held in honor by all, and let the marriage bed be kept undefiled; for God will judge fornicators and adulterers. ⁵ Keep your lives free from the love of money, and be content with what you have; for he has said, "I will never leave you or forsake you." ⁶ So we can say with confidence, "The Lord is my helper; I will not be afraid. What can anyone do to me?" — Hebrews 13:1-6

Talk about big shoes to fill! Joshua had the tall order of succeeding Moses as the leader of the covenant people. How would you like that assignment? First of all, leading any group of people, no matter who they are, is a formidable task. But following a legend like Moses makes the task seem even more intimidating.

I ought to know. When I became senior pastor in 2009, I was succeeding Jim Wooten, who had served this church for twenty-one years — longer than any other pastor in our church's history. Not only had Jim served this congregation long, he had served this congregation well. It was all the work of God, of course — but from a human standpoint, Jim helped revitalize our church at a crucial time when our church was struggling to survive. For the last seven years of Jim's tenure here, I was privileged to serve this church as associate pastor. And whenever Jim was away on vacation or on his sabbatical, I kept the letters "WWJD" before me at all times: *What would Jim do?*

Now of course, I ultimately wanted to do what the other J, the main J, was leading me to do. But so often in trying to discern what Jesus would do, I asked myself what Jim would do, and usually found that there was an amazing consistency between what Jesus would do and what Jim would do. I cannot tell you how many times during those seven years I heard Jim say of his work as pastor, "This is an impossible job." So you can imagine my utter fright when, on his last Sunday as pastor of Earle Street, he called the staff up in front of the congregation, handed me a baton, and said, "Don't drop it." Because I was following a legend, the bar had been raised high. I was being called to do what the legend himself called an impossible job. I was being handed a baton and publicly commanded not to drop it. And if you don't think I was intimidated, you don't know me very well.

Add to that intimidating impossibility the people I was being called to lead. That would be you. So throw "you" into the mix, and now you really have a perfect storm. Just kidding, but not really. It is not that you are rebellious, complaining, whining people like the people Moses was called to lead. It is not that you are difficult individuals (for the most part). It is just that you are all so very different from each other — politically, theologically, denominationally, socio-economically. Individually, you are some of the most wonderful people I have ever known — but putting you all together with your different ideas and trying to make progress is quite a challenge. One of the hardest parts of my job is to keep us all united and focused on what matters the most. We all agree that God is love, that Jesus is Lord, and that we should love God, love our neighbors, and make disciples. We all agree on our mission as a church. We all know where we are going, but we do not always agree on how to get there.

So when the book of Joshua begins, I am feeling his pain. The Lord says to Joshua, "Moses is gone; and now it is up to you to finish what Moses started, and lead my people all the way into the Promised Land." Joshua had been with the people the entire way through the years of wilderness wanderings and the times of testing. He had witnessed first-hand the complaining and rebellion, the whining and the disobedience. He had seen what a hard time Moses had managing these people. And he knew what an extraordinary leader Moses had been. And if Moses couldn't get the people into the Promised Land, he had to wonder if he had what it took to lead them in the last stretch of their long journey. But the Lord continued: "Moses is dead … as I was with Moses, so I will be with you; I will not fail you or forsake you" (Joshua 1:2a, 5b).

In these uncertain, unsettling, unprecedented times, I believe that God's word to Joshua back then is God's word to us all right now. We are here. We may wish we were somewhere else. We may long for the good old days. We may whine and complain, we may cast blame and become resentful. We may feel hopeless or helpless, lost or alone. We may not know exactly how we got here or where we are going from here. But God's promise is the same now as it was then: "I will be with you; I will not fail you or forsake you." "You may be here," God said, "but so am I."

At the very end of the letter to the Hebrews, which is more like a sermon than a letter, the writer offers a series of concluding admonitions, some parting advice and timely reminders. In chapter 13, the writer gives a passionate appeal to the readers to practice Christian morality and to worship and work with an unchanging Christ in a constantly changing world. "Let mutual love continue," he wrote. "Do not neglect to show hospitality to strangers … Remember those who are in prison … and those who are ill-treated … Let marriage be held in honor among all … Keep your life free from love of money and be content with what you have" (Hebrews 13:1-3).

And then, after presenting these challenges, he repeated the promise that God gave Joshua: "I will never fail you nor forsake you." Then he quotes from Psalm 118:6: "The Lord is my helper, I will not be afraid; what can anyone do to me?" In other words, if God is with us and will never forsake us, then no matter where we happen to be at any given moment or season in time, we are not alone. And if God will never fail us, then there is nothing anyone can do to us that will matter in the end.

John Ortberg shares a story about meeting a young boy while he was surfing. He said there was no one else in the water. In fact, there was no one around at all, except a guy the size of Goliath doing tae kwon do on the beach. This is how he described it:

> After I'd been out a little while, a tiny wisp of a kid came paddling up out of nowhere — I couldn't believe he was out there by himself. He pulled his little board right up next to mine. He was so small he hardly needed a board. He could have stood up in the ocean on a Frisbee.

Anyway, he started chatting with me like we were old friends. He told me his name was Shane. He asked me how long I'd been surfing. I asked him how long he'd been surfing. "Seven years," he said. "How old are you?" I asked. "Eight." He asked me about my kids and my family. Then he said, "What I like about surfing is that it's so peaceful. You meet a lot of nice people here." "You're a nice guy, Shane," I said. "That's why you meet nice people."

We talked a while longer. Then I asked him, "How did you get here, Shane?" "My dad brought me," he said. Then he turned around and waved at the nearly empty beach. The Goliath doing martial arts waved back. "Hi, Son," he called out. Then I knew why Shane was so at home in the ocean. It wasn't his size. It wasn't his skill. It was who was sitting on the beach. His father was always watching. And his father was very big.[30]

Shane could feel secure about venturing out as long as he knew his father was with him. As long as he could see his father and his father could see him, as long as they never got out of each other's sight, Shane was never alone. And neither are we. Wherever we happen to be in any given moment, God is with us. God is always close enough to us to be able to see us. We could never venture, or wander, so far that we could ever escape God's presence with us. We may find ourselves in a broken, fearful, fallen world. But we are not here alone.

The second truth that Shane realized was that his father was very big — bigger than anything that could harm him, bigger than the

---

30 John Ortberg. *I'd Like You More If You Were More Like Me: Getting Real About Getting Close* (Carol Stream, Illinois: Tyndale Momentum, 2017), 65-66.

problems that he had, bigger than the dangers that lurked beneath the ocean, bigger than anything that could threaten his ultimate security. It was not just that his father was with him, but it was also that his father was big enough to take care of any challenge or danger he had to face. God's promise to Joshua was not just that He would be with him and would not abandon, forsake, or leave him. But God's promise was that God would not *fail* him either. The Hebrew word for *fail* means to drop or let go of, become helpless, or fall limp. When the writer of Hebrews quotes that Old Testament verse, he uses the Greek word which is often translated "leave." In fact, that is the way many of us have memorized this verse: "I will never leave you nor forsake you." But the Greek word actually means to loosen or let go, to fail to uphold, to unfasten." The two-fold promise is not just that God is with us, but that God is stronger than anything that could loosen us, and bigger than any danger or challenge that could threaten us.

An old gospel song by Gordon Jensen came back to me as I thought about the bigness of our God who will never fail us. The words go like this:

> *Bigger than all my problems, bigger than all my fears, bigger than all my questions, bigger than all the shadows that fall across my path, bigger than all the confusion, bigger than anything, bigger than all the giants of fear and unbelief, bigger than all my hang-ups, God is bigger than any mountain that I can or cannot see.*[31]

God is bigger ... infinitely bigger than anything we could imagine.

The story is told of a woman who came to G. Campbell Morgan and

---

31 Gordon Jensen. *Bigger Than Any Mountain*. Copyright © 1976 New Spring Publishing Inc. (ASCAP) (adm. at CapitolCMGPublishing.com) All rights reserved. Used by permission.

said, "I only take the big things to God. I don't take the little things to God."

G. Campbell Morgan looked at her and said, "Anything you take to God is little." Anything we take to God is little compared to God, even if it is big to us.[32]

It was that promise that sustained Joshua as he led the covenant people from where they were into the future that God had in store for them. It was not just that God was watching, but that God was very big. And the same promise that God gave to Joshua reverberated through the centuries so that the writer of Hebrews would pick up on it and repeat it in a new time to a different people. And now centuries after that, in these unsettling times, the promise of God is still the same. And if we will put our trust in God, we will be able to venture out into the vast ocean that we call life, secure that there, no matter how far or how deep we go, God will still be there with us and for us — and even when we let go of God, God will not let go of us. Now that is a promise that will see us all the way through this life to the next and will be the theme of our song through endless ages. Even when we fail and forsake God, God will never fail nor forsake us. Amen.

---

32 Tony Evans. *Tony Evans' Book of Illustrations: Stories, Quotes and Anecdotes* (Chicago: Moody Press, 2009), 234.

Sing Your Way Home

LAMENTATIONS 1:1-6; PSALM 137

¹ *How lonely sits the city*
that once was full of people!
How like a widow she has become,
she that was great among the nations!
She that was a princess among the provinces
has become a vassal.

² *She weeps bitterly in the night,*
with tears on her cheeks;
among all her lovers
she has no one to comfort her;
all her friends have dealt treacherously with her,
they have become her enemies.

³ *Judah has gone into exile with suffering*
and hard servitude;
she lives now among the nations,
and finds no resting place;
her pursuers have all overtaken her
in the midst of her distress.

⁴ *The roads to Zion mourn,*
for no one comes to the festivals;

all her gates are desolate,
her priests groan;
her young girls grieve,[a]
and her lot is bitter.

⁵ *Her foes have become the masters,*
her enemies prosper,
because the Lord has made her suffer
for the multitude of her transgressions;
her children have gone away,
captives before the foe.

⁶ *From daughter Zion has departed*
all her majesty.
Her princes have become like stags
that find no pasture;
they fled without strength
before the pursuer.
— Lamentations 1:1-6

¹ *By the rivers of Babylon —*
there we sat down and there we wept
when we remembered Zion.
² *On the willows there*
we hung up our harps.
³ *For there our captors*
asked us for songs,
and our tormentors asked for mirth, saying,
"Sing us one of the songs of Zion!"

> [4] *How could we sing the Lord's song*
> *in a foreign land?*
> [5] *If I forget you, O Jerusalem,*
> *let my right hand wither!*
> [6] *Let my tongue cling to the roof of my mouth,*
> *if I do not remember you,*
> *if I do not set Jerusalem*
> *above my highest joy.*
>
> [7] *Remember, O Lord, against the Edomites*
> *the day of Jerusalem's fall,*
> *how they said, "Tear it down! Tear it down!*
> *Down to its foundations!"*
> [8] *O daughter Babylon, you devastator!*
> *Happy shall they be who pay you back*
> *what you have done to us!*
> [9] *Happy shall they be who take your little ones*
> *and dash them against the rock!*
> — Psalm 137

"There is no place like home." Do you remember the girl with the ruby slippers who clicked her shoes together as she repeated that line over and over? Who could forget Dorothy, the little girl from Kansas, who had a dream about being away from home? And what a dream it was! A dream filled with action, adventure, suspense, and drama. But lurking beneath the surface of the dream was the constant desire of a little farm girl to return to the stability and security of her home in Kansas. One of the striking things about Dorothy's journey was that she and her companions sang along the way. Somehow, singing made the yellow-brick road seem brighter. No matter how dark and frightening her life became, Dorothy sang her way home.

The difference between Dorothy and us is that we do not live in a dream world. The world in which we live is real. There are no magical slippers that we can click together so that everything can be made right again. Have you ever been at a place in your life when there was nowhere you could call home? Or perhaps you were still at home, but it was not the same anymore? Have you ever wondered where God was and what God was doing, why God allowed certain things to happen, why God did not help you then, or why God will not help you now? Do you ever find yourself remembering the good old days and longing for their return? Whether you are still at home and things are not the same anymore, or you have been forced to leave the familiarity and security of your home, it is easy to feel angry and bitter, resentful and confused, depressed and discouraged.

The Bible has a word which conjures up all those images and feelings. The word is *exile*. And we do not have to be in a foreign land to be there. It is possible to be in exile in your own home. Exile occurs when you feel abandoned. Exile is being cut off from the past and everything you hold dear. Exile is dreading the unknown future. Exile is a time when God seems to be at least silent, maybe even absent, or even worse, unconcerned. Nothing makes sense when you are in exile. Exile is facing up to the stark reality that some of the dreams which have propelled you for so long are never going to be fulfilled.

One of the darkest, most dreadful times in the history of God's people was that period of time in the sixth century BC known as the Babylonian exile, when the Babylonians, with the help and encouragement of the Edomites, destroyed the temple and the holy city of Jerusalem. Some of Judah's peasants were left in the land of Judah to mourn the destruction of all that was sacred to them, while the more affluent and productive people of Judah were taken by the

Babylonians against their will into exile to a place that was distant and foreign to them in every way. It is hard to know which would have been worse: to be in exile at home or to be in exile in a foreign land. The Scripture passages we have read today help us get in touch with the emotional intensity of the people who were left in Judah and those who were taken into captivity. The poet of Lamentations was looking at the devastation and destruction from the standpoint of those who were left in Judah. The tone of the opening poem in chapter 1 is utter sorrow. Where do you even start to rebuild a life that has literally been reduced to ashes? There was nothing to do but grieve. It is true that at least they were still in their homeland. But life was never going to be the same again for them. Hear again the lamentations of the poet:

> How lonely sits the city that once was full of people! How like a widow she has become ... She weeps bitterly in the night, with tears on her cheeks ... [but] she has no one to comfort her. [Even] the roads to Zion mourn ... all her gates are desolate, her priests groan, her young girls grieve, and her lot is bitter ... Her foes have become the masters, her enemies prosper, because the Lord has made her suffer for the multitude of her transgressions; her children have gone away, captives before the foe.

The poet of Psalm 137 was looking at the exile from the standpoint of those who had been taken into captivity in Babylon, where they were forced to learn a new language, adapt to a new culture, and adjust to a whole new way of life. Haunted by the memories of their tragedy, stripped of their dignity, and ridiculed by the taunts of their captors, they wept until they could weep no more. But soon their sorrow turned to anger, and their tears to rage. Their frustration soon turned into violent hatred, and their grief into bitterness. Why can't things be like they used to be? The people of God wept as they recalled the time, not too long ago, when Jerusalem was a thriving center of religion. Now it lay in ruins. They remembered the splendor of the temple, the house of God, the unique place of God's presence. Now it had been reduced to a pile of rocks. They had been uprooted from the very land which God had given to them and had been taken as hostages to a foreign land. The harps which once had been used in temple worship were now hung on the poplar trees in Babylon as vivid reminders of the songs they used to sing. As if their grief were not intense enough, they were given no privacy. They could not even mourn in peace. Their cruel captors made sport of their grief, demanding that they sing one of their songs now. "Sing one of those songs you used to sing in the temple. Let's hear your music now." The cruel demands of their captors drove the iron even deeper into their sad hearts. The mere thought of one of those special songs reminded them of the splendor, beauty, and security of the Jerusalem temple.

That kind of ridicule is enough to turn sorrow into rage. How could they sing the LORD's song in a foreign land? How could they be expected to pick up their harps again and sing the songs they used to sing under these circumstances? They had no heart for music and song. The last thing in the world they felt like doing was singing one of those songs now. To sing one of the old songs now would be more painful than joyful. This psalmist would have rather died than give his captors the pleasure of hearing the LORD's song.

This psalm presents a brutally frank picture of human nature — how quickly human emotions can degenerate if left unchecked. The more we think about and dwell on our tragedies and failures, the more intense and destructive our emotions can become. What starts out as tears of grief can end up as curses of vengeance. The psalmist never reached a point at which he could put the past behind him. In fact, that is a problem many of us have. The past often has a way of paralyzing us. There are harps hanging on every tree — stark reminders everywhere we turn of the way things used to be, of the hopes and dreams that have been shattered, of the new realities that will never go away. It is true that life may never be the same again, but life can still be good. For we worship and serve One who transcends geography, culture, and circumstances. Even in exile, God gives us a song to sing — and, by faith, we can sing that song together all the way home.

Some would say this is just denial. This is just self-deception. This is just a bunch of positive-thinking, mental gymnastics. This is just talking ourselves into believing that things are really not as bad as they seem. This is just making the best of a bad situation. But if exile teaches us anything at all, it teaches us that God really is present even in our agony and grief. God is actively involved even in our tragedies to achieve a divine purpose for us. God gives us a song to sing even when we are in exile.

That's what Dorothy and her companions did. And along the way, she discovered that she had been home all along. Dorothy learned what some of us are still learning — that home is not a place, but a person. When she was away from home, the one picture she could not get out of her mind was the picture of Auntie Em beckoning her to come home. Dorothy never got so far away that she could not see that face, if only through a glass darkly — and hear that voice calling her by name, if only as a whisper.

As followers of Jesus, we remember that dark and dreadful night when Jesus gathered in an upper room with His disciples and warned them of things to come. He told them that life would never be the same again. They were about to face their own exile, but they would not have to face it alone. Jesus took bread and wine, shared it with them, and reminded them that, even though He would not be present with them in the same way, they would always have a home in Him and with Him. Then before they went out into the darkest of all nights, they sang. Still today, Christians all over the world are singing that song. And by faith, even in exile, we will sing it all the way home. Amen.

SERMONS FOR
SPECIAL OCCASIONS

As Slow as Christmas
An Advent Sermon

JEREMIAH 33:14-16

> ^{14} *The days are surely coming, says the Lord, when I will fulfill the promise I made to the house of Israel and the house of Judah.* ^{15} *In those days and at that time I will cause a righteous Branch to spring up for David; and he shall execute justice and righteousness in the land.* ^{16} *In those days Judah will be saved and Jerusalem will live in safety. And this is the name by which it will be called: "The Lord is our righteousness."*

My father used to have a saying that I find myself using frequently myself. When something was supposed to happen, and didn't; or when he had to wait in line or wait for his meals to be served to him on a silver platter; or when people told him they were going to do something, but didn't stop and do it right then, my father used to say, "They are slow as Christmas."

Now that I am all grown up, it seems like Christmas comes too *fast* every year. But when we were children, it seemed like Christmas was never going to get here. I remember saying to my father, "I can't wait until Christmas," to which he would reply, "Oh, yeah, you can wait. You can and you will." And so, as children, we begin to learn the art of waiting. And some of us never learn. Waiting can be one of the hardest disciplines we ever practice, especially if we have bought into what someone Sue Monk Kidd called a "quickaholic spirituality":

Complex life issues are routinely introduced, dealt with, and solved in neat sixty-minute segments on television ... . We're surrounded by express lanes, express mail, express credit. There aren't just restaurants, but "fast-food" restaurants; not simply markets, but "jiffy" markets. Faster is better. Ask most anyone ... . We live in an age of acceleration, in an era so seduced by the instantaneous that we're in grave danger of losing our ability to wait. Life moves at a staggering pace. Computers yield up immediate answers. Pictures develop before our eyes. Satellites beam television signals from practically anywhere, allowing far-away images to appear instantly in our living rooms.[33]

Whether we are waiting on Christmas or something else, waiting is an art that many of us have not yet mastered. But considering how much of our lives we spend waiting, it might be important for us to learn how to wait for some eventualities that are "as slow as Christmas."

All of us are waiting on something. If it is nothing more than waiting on this sermon to be over, we're waiting on something. Some of us are waiting to see if anyone or the right one will ask us out on a date, or waiting for that important football game. Some of us are waiting on a big test at school, or waiting to get our driver's license. Some of us are waiting to see if we will get accepted into the college of our choice. Some of us are waiting to get a big promotion at work. Some are waiting to get financially stable. Some are waiting on a particular crisis to run its course so we can resume a so-called "normal" life (whatever that is). Some are waiting for retirement. Some of us are waiting for Mr. or Ms. Right to come along and sweep us off our feet. Some of us are waiting for that

---

33 Sue Monk Kidd, *When the Heart Waits: Spiritual Direction for Life's Sacred Questions* (San Francisco, 1992), 21-23.

first baby to come. Some are waiting for a relationship to be reconciled. Some of us are waiting for our children to grow out of this phase they are in. Some are waiting to be married; some are waiting to be divorced. Some are waiting for the results of the biopsy. Some are waiting for our grief to run its course. And some of us, frankly, are waiting to die. But all of us are waiting for something. Waiting and hoping are twins. One calls for the other. And both require patience and endurance.

As a pastor, I have spent many hours in so-called "waiting rooms," special places set aside for people to sit and wait. You can learn so much by watching people wait, and the one experience that seems to be common to most people who wait is the feeling of helplessness. If we could help, if we could make things happen, or make things better, we would take matters into our own hands, and then we would not have to wait. But waiting is all about acknowledging our limitations. It is all about drawing an imaginary line in our souls and distinguishing between the things we can control and the things we cannot, the things that can be done now, and the things that will have to wait. Waiting is about learning to live with mystery, to dwell in unknowing, to live inside a question and coexist with the tensions of uncertainty. Waiting involves a willingness to incubate pain and let it birth something new.[34]

Centuries before the first Christmas, the prophet Jeremiah spoke on behalf of God and promised that there would be a descendant from the line of King David, who would be not just a King, but a Savior, who would execute justice and righteousness in the land. They certainly would not have used this term to describe what they were waiting for, but what they were waiting for was Christmas, the coming of a Messiah, God's Anointed One. But Jeremiah was not the first or the

---

34 Ibid.

only prophet to make such a promise. In fact, generations had already lived and died without that promise ever having been fulfilled. And even though Jeremiah was repeating that promise for a new generation, the fulfillment of that promise would still be centuries away. It would literally be as "slow as Christmas." For us, Christmas is never more than a year away — but for them, Christmas was centuries away. Centuries! And frankly, some of us can relate. We have heard God's promises for so long, and yet the realities of our lives do not seem to budge. And many of us feel as if we will not live to see the day when God's promise is fulfilled. So what good does it do to wait for something that we will not live to see?

In the summer of 2011, a mission team from our church went to one of the most depressed pockets of poverty in West Virginia. Unemployment was seventy percent. There were no jobs to be had. And everywhere we turned, there were people in poverty, doing nothing to make their lives better. At one point, someone in another group said, "Everywhere I turn, all I see is laziness." And someone else in our group said, "What you are seeing is not laziness. What you are seeing is hopelessness."

Sue Monk Kidd tells of a time when she went to a monastery for a retreat. She said that one morning, after morning prayers, she walked to the edge of a pond and sat on the grass. She was trying to just be still and wait in the moment — but almost instantly, her inner chaos rose up. The need to keep moving to act, to solve everything, overpowered her, and she got to her feet. As she returned to her guest quarters, she noticed a monk, ski cap pulled over his ears, sitting perfectly still beneath a tree. She said there was such reverence in his silhouette, such tranquil sturdiness, that she paused to watch. He was the picture of waiting. Later, she sought him out and said, "I saw you today sitting beneath the tree — just sitting there so still. How is it that you can wait so patiently in the moment? I can't seem to get used to the idea of doing nothing."

The monk broke into a wonderful grin and said, "Well, there's the problem right there, young lady. You've bought into the cultural myth that when you're waiting you're doing nothing." Then he took his hands and placed them on her shoulders, peered straight into her eyes and said, "I hope you'll hear what I am about to tell you. I hope you'll hear it all the way down to your toes. When you're waiting, you're *not* doing nothing. You're doing the most important something there is. You're allowing your soul to grow up. If you can't be still and wait, you can't become what God created you to be."[35]

One Saturday morning in December, I woke up fairly early and planned to have breakfast with one of my brothers and his wife and my mother, and then spend the rest of the day at home, leisurely helping to decorate the house for Christmas. About 8:45 a.m., I heard a little bell coming from my computer alerting me that I had an appointment on my calendar. For a long time, I have had a recurring nightmare that I was supposed to do a funeral or a wedding or a worship service, and all these people were waiting for me to get there. But, for some reason, I couldn't get there. Either I was lost and couldn't find my way there; or I was delayed for some reason; or I was there, but couldn't find my sermon. Anyway, yesterday, my nightmare came true. At 8:45 a.m., my computer alerted me that I was supposed to be teaching at Erskine at 9:00, and Due West is an hour away from my house. Somehow, I had it in my mind that it was the *next* Saturday. I stared at my computer in disbelief. And then started saying over and over and again with increasing intensity, "Oh, no! Oh, no! Oh, no!" Sylvia came running into the room, thinking I was having a heart attack. I thought I was, too!

---

35 Ibid., 21-22.

I gathered my school stuff as fast as I could and headed to the metropolitan area of Due West. You really can't get to Due West from my house, especially not fast. I couldn't find any of my students' cell phone numbers to tell them I would be late. But eventually, one of them called me to see if there was a problem. I explained the situation and told them I would be about an hour late. I exceeded the speed limit and got there as fast as I could. I parked my car and rushed to the seminary building, expressing my embarrassment and apologizing profusely. They were all locked out of the building, sitting peacefully in the rocking chairs on the front porch, just shooting the breeze. One of them said, "Don't apologize. We are always rushing in and out of class, and never have a chance to get to know each other. Thanks for making us wait." About that time, another student came rushing across the street from the library saying, "You saved me today. I was not ready to make my presentation to the class today. But that extra hour saved me. Thanks for making us wait." And in that moment, I was reminded of what I planned to say to you today. When you are waiting, you do not have to do nothing. Waiting can be productive.

If the season of Advent teaches us nothing else, it teaches us that there is no shortcut to joy. Sometimes we achieve our deepest progress standing still. Sometimes we must go inward before we can go forward. Waiting calls us to be in this moment or this season of our lives, without leaning so far into the future that we tear our roots from the present.[36] And of course, the hardest part about waiting is that it is unresolved. It means giving up control over our future and trusting God to open that path before us that we cannot see. Waiting is a reminder that we are not in control. And some of us desperately need to be reminded of that.

---

36 Ibid.

Hope is what makes our waiting meaningful and purposeful. Hope takes the long view. In fact, it believes what it cannot even see. As Paul said in the letter to the Romans: "Now hope that is seen is not hope. For who hopes for what is seen? But if we hope for what we do not see, we wait for it with patience." There is no fast-food version of hope. There is no McHope. That is because God is not just a rescuer. God is also a midwife, One who comes to be with us in our pain, to wait with us.[37] And something very important can happen to us and in us when we are waiting *for* God and waiting *with* God.

As it turned out, the people of Jeremiah's day would never see their hopes and dreams fulfilled. They lived and died waiting on the Lord. But Jeremiah would want us to know, and Paul would affirm, that there is no better way to live or die than waiting on the Lord. In fact, there is a sense in which we all will die waiting for God's promises to be fulfilled. But in the meantime, between promise and fulfillment, between hope and joy, when we are waiting for God, we are *not* doing *nothing*. We are allowing our souls to grow up and we are becoming the people God created us to be. When God says, "Wait," God has something in store for us worth waiting for that is as slow, but as sure, as Christmas. Amen.

---

37 Ibid.

Getting the Christmas Story Right

A Christmas Sermon

JOHN 3:16

For God so loved the world that he gave his only Son, so that everyone who believes in him may not perish but may have eternal life.

We all look for ways to simplify the mystery of our faith. Take my aunt "Wee Wee," for example. I always like to let people know that the reason we called her "Wee Wee" is that we couldn't say, "Louise," and "Wee Wee" was the best we could do. Anyway, when I was a student in seminary, "Wee Wee" would fix lunch for me once a week. And I guess my uncle Grady thought that, because I was a student in seminary, I could answer all his theological questions. One day, he asked me if the Bible says that God will forgive our sins and remember them no more. I told him yes. Then he asked why the Bible says we are still going to have to give an account of all our sins if God has already forgiven them.

I used the answer that Marshall Sargent always taught me to use, "There are many views on that" (which actually meant I didn't have a clue — and still don't).

Anyway, "Wee Wee" was quick to jump into the conversation and rescue me. "Oh, Grady," she said, "just believe in the Lord Jesus Christ and you will be saved. Now eat your cornbread."

We all look for ways to simplify the mystery of our faith. I am reminded of the late Karl Barth, arguably one of the greatest theologians of the twentieth century. Dr. Barth wrote a massive, ten-volume work called *Church Dogmatics*. He was a scholar and a professor, and was respected all over the world for his contribution to Christian theology. The story is told that, once when Dr. Barth was asked to summarize his theology in a simple statement, he thought for a moment and said, "Jesus loves me. This I know for the Bible tells me so." We all look for ways to simplify the mystery of our faith. And what we do for the Christian faith in general, we do for the Christmas story in particular.

I cannot remember or find the source of this illustration, but once a Sunday School teacher asked a group of first graders to write the Christmas story as they remembered it. This is the story that one of the first graders wrote:

> In those days, the guy who invented Caesar salads got a degree. And all the people had to pay their taxes. Even Mary and Joseph had to pay. But the angel said, "Fear not. You can afford it." But they couldn't. They couldn't even afford a motel room. So they stayed in a barn, which was a good place for the shepherds to bring their sheep. Mary was so big that she had to wear waddling clothes. When Jesus was finally born, the men who were supposed to be wise got lost and had to stop and ask directions. Finally, they found Jesus — but when they got there, everybody was afraid because they brought Frankenstein with them. So the angels came again and said, "Fear not."

Well, sometimes it is hard to keep the details of the Christmas story straight. But John's Gospel makes it easy for us. Many of us learned it as a child. Martin Luther is often credited as having called it "the gospel in miniature." And even if we can't get the rest of the Christmas story straight, if we can just remember that one verse, then we have it all. I like to think of John 3:16 as John's Christmas story.

Usually we spend more time in Matthew and Luke during the Advent/Christmas season. After all, they are the ones who tell us the Christmas story in the most familiar ways. Mark, the first of the Gospel writers, skipped the story of Jesus's birth altogether. The Gospel of Mark begins with the ministry of John the Baptizer — and when Jesus first appears, He is already a grown man coming to John to be baptized. Matthew begins his Gospel by giving us the genealogy of Jesus Christ, tracing his roots all the way back to Abraham, the father of the Jews.

And against that backdrop, Matthew tells us the familiar story of Jesus's birth, beginning with Joseph's dilemma and the angel's appearance to Joseph to reassure him that God was at work. Matthew tells us of the wise men who followed the star from the east to worship the king of the Jews and bring Him their gifts of gold, frankincense, and myrrh. Matthew then tells us how Herod felt threatened by a potential rival to his throne, and Joseph and Mary fled to Egypt with their newborn Son until the coast was clear. Luke, on the other hand, begins the story by introducing an elderly couple who had no children: a priest named Zechariah and his wife, Elizabeth, who gave birth to a son who came to be known as John the Baptizer. In the sixth month of Elizabeth's pregnancy, Elizabeth's cousin, Mary, also received an announcement from an angel that she, too, would bear a son, whose name would be called Jesus. And even though she had no husband at the time, she praised God and accepted God's plan.

It was Luke who told us about the decree from Caesar Augustus, the shepherds who came to Bethlehem to see the Christ Child, the circumcision of Jesus on the eighth day, Mary and Joseph's sacrifice in the temple, the old man in Jerusalem named Simeon who had been waiting so long for the Messiah, and the eighty-four-year-old female preacher,

Anna, who also joined in the celebration of Jesus's birth. Luke then gives us his version of the genealogy of Jesus which goes back farther than Abraham, the father of Jews. Luke traces the genealogy of Jesus all the way back to Adam, to show that Jesus came not just for the Jews, but for all of humanity.

But John, writing at a later time for a different audience and for different reasons, begins his account of the Gospel by going as far back as he could go — farther than Abraham, even farther than Adam — all the way back. In fact, he begins his account of the Gospel with the same words with which the Hebrew Scriptures begin: "In the beginning …" John wants us to know that the story of Jesus begins not with the appearance of a Child in Bethlehem, but with God in the very beginning. In fact, John wants us to know that the historical Jesus is not just the Son of God, but God in the flesh. "In the beginning was the Word," John wrote. "And the Word was with God and the Word was God … and the Word became flesh and dwelt among us" (John 1:1, 14). The Word through whom the world was spoken into existence, the Word which was in the beginning with God, the Word who was God, became a historical person bound by time and space. In Jesus Christ, the eternal Word became flesh. That is the majestic and poetic way John begins his Christmas story in chapter 1.

But it is not until chapter 3 that John presents the Christmas story in a single, simple verse that even a child can learn and understand. In chapter 3 of John's Gospel, Jesus had a night time visit with Nicodemus, a member of the Jewish ruling council. The earlier half of the chapter features a dialogue between Jesus and His visitor, which was a most revealing conversation in its own right. But by the time we reach verse 16, dialogue has turned to monologue and Nicodemus may as well have vanished back into the night. The stage was set for John to present the Christmas story in a simple sentence.

And the sentence begins with **the reality of God's love**. The verse begins where everything begins — with God. The Bible never explains or defends the existence of God. There are no arguments in the Bible for belief in God such as you might find in handbooks of apologetics, theology, and philosophy. The Bible assumes without question the reality of God and simply dismisses as foolish those who deny the existence of God. There is a simplicity in John's Gospel that is striking. God is real.

But just the assumption or declaration of God's existence is not necessarily good news by itself. It is important to know the nature and character of God — God's attitude toward us — before we can receive God's existence as good news. That is why the next part of the verse is so crucial. Our faith rises or falls not just on the existence of God, but on the character of God. "God so *loved* …" In the New Testament, the Greek word for love, *agape*, is applied in specific ways to the love of God in Jesus Christ — the pure, unmerited, persistent, overflowing, creative, redemptive, unconditional love of God. In another of John's writings, John goes even farther to say that God not only *has* love, and *gives* love, but God *is* love.

And how you hear that speaks volumes about what you believe about God and yourself. Some people find it hard to believe that God is love, and some people find it hard to believe that they are lovable. Some people have been conditioned to believe that God is a harsh slave driver who makes no allowances for brokenness and sin, an enemy whose favor we must win.[38] And some people have been conditioned to believe that, because they are broken and sinful, not even God could find a way to love them unconditionally. Maybe you don't feel very loved. Maybe you don't feel very lovable. Maybe you don't feel very lovely. But the good

---

38 Charles E. Poole. *Don't Cry Past Tuesday: Hopeful Words for Difficult Days* (Macon, Georgia: Smyth and Helwys Publishing, Inc., 1991), 22.

news of Christmas is that love is more than a feeling. Some things are real and true even when we do not happen to feel like they are true. This verse assumes and affirms the reality of God's love.

This verse also shows us **the scope of God's love**. It was the world, the cosmos, the entire created order, that God so loved. It was not just a nation; it was not just the good people; it was not only the people who loved Him; it was the world. The unlovable and the unlovely, the lonely who have no one else to love them, the ones who love God and the ones who never even think of God, those who rest in the love of God and those who spurn it. All are included in this vast, inclusive love of God. But God's love is not just cosmic; it is personal. It is not just for the world; it is for you. Thought I cannot verify the source of this quotation, Saint Augustine is often credited as saying, "God loves each one of us as if there were only one of us to love."

This verse also shows us **the purpose of God's love**: to offer eternal life. The next verse, verse 17, says it another way: that God sent His Son into the world not to judge or condemn the world, but to save the world. This truth is why Jesus could say to a woman caught in the very act of adultery, "I do not condemn you; go, and do not sin again." This truth is why Paul could write to the Romans: "There is therefore now no condemnation for those who are in Christ Jesus." The purpose of God's love is not to judge the world, but to give eternal life to and save those who believe.

But finally, this verse shows us **the depth of God's love.** When God loved, God loved the whole world — and when God gave, God gave His only Son. And that is what makes this verse a Christmas story in and of itself. God didn't just love the world from a safe, sentimental distance. God's love is not just an attitude, but an action. It is not a vague sentiment, but a personal gift. That is what we celebrate this season of the year — God's love Gift to the world, the gift of God's unique Son, indeed the Gift of God's own Self. Here we see that the Gift and the Giver are indistinguishable. The initiative was with God. The action originated with God. It was not a passive kind of love. It was not just a warm feeling of affection in the heart of God; it was an action of God. It was a Gift from God. In fact, the Gift *was* God.

So you might not get all the details of the Christmas story straight. But if you get this much, you have it all: "God so loved the world that He gave His only begotten Son that whosoever believeth in Him should not perish but have everlasting life." This verse is the good news of the gospel, the good news of Christmas. God's love is not a vague sentimental feeling. God's love is a Gift that you may unwrap by believing in Jesus. God's love is life for you — life that is abundant and life that is eternal. Merry Christmas! Amen.

He Appeared Also to Me

An Easter Sermon

1 CORINTHIANS 15:1-11

¹ *Now I would remind you, brothers and sisters, of the good news that I proclaimed to you, which you in turn received, in which also you stand,* ² *through which also you are being saved, if you hold firmly to the message that I proclaimed to you — unless you have come to believe in vain.*

³ *For I handed on to you as of first importance what I in turn had received: that Christ died for our sins in accordance with the scriptures,* ⁴ *and that he was buried, and that he was raised on the third day in accordance with the scriptures,* ⁵ *and that he appeared to Cephas, then to the twelve.* ⁶ *Then he appeared to more than five hundred brothers and sisters at one time, most of whom are still alive, though some have died.* ⁷ *Then he appeared to James, then to all the apostles.* ⁸ *Last of all, as to one untimely born, he appeared also to me.* ⁹ *For I am the least of the apostles, unfit to be called an apostle, because I persecuted the church of God.* ¹⁰ *But by the grace of God I am what I am, and his grace toward me has not been in vain. On the contrary, I worked harder than any of them — though it was not I, but the grace of God that is with me.* ¹¹ *Whether then it was I or they, so we proclaim and so you have come to believe.*

Will Willimon tells the story of a time when he was a pastor and visited a dying man whom the doctors had given only a couple of days to live. Dr. Willimon asked the man what he was feeling, and if he was fearful. "No," the man said, "I am not fearful because of my faith in Jesus."

Willimon replied with a predictable pastoral response: "It's good that you know that you belong to Christ, and your future is in God's hands."

But the man replied, almost as if to correct his pastor (and pastors often need correcting): "I'm not hopeful because of what I believe about the *future*. I'm hopeful because of what I have experienced in the past." Dr. Willimon asked him to say more. And the man said, "I look back over my life, all the mistakes I've made, all the times I've turned away from Jesus, gone my own way, strayed, and got lost. And time and again, He found a way to get to me, showed up and got me, looked for me when I wasn't looking for Him. And I don't think He'll let something like my dying defeat His love for me."

And then Willimon concluded, "Now there's a man who understands Easter."[39]

Writing some twenty-five or thirty years after the time of the historical Jesus, Paul had been the founding pastor of the church in Corinth. Sometime after leaving Corinth, he learned of some problems in the dysfunctional Corinthian church, and wrote this letter that we now call First Corinthians to address some of their moral, ethical, and practical issues. But it was not until the end of the letter that Paul addressed the only theological issue that apparently was a concern for the Corinthians: the issue of the resurrection. He began his response by passing along to *them* a creed that had been indirectly passed along to *him* presumably through the disciples who were the first to see the risen

---

39 William H. Willimon. *The Collected Sermons of William H. Willimon* (Louisville: Westminster John Knox Press, 2010), 252.

Jesus. Most New Testament interpreters recognize this ancient creed that begins in verse 3b as possibly the oldest text in the New Testament in its original form:

> *Christ died for our sins in accordance with the Scriptures. He was buried. He was raised on the third day in accordance with the Scriptures. He appeared to Cephas, to the twelve, to more than 500 people at one time, to James and all the apostles.*

These are the stories we usually read and hear on Easter Day. The Gospels state that the risen Jesus first appeared to three women, among them Mary. The second recorded appearance of the risen Jesus occurred on Easter afternoon as two disciples of Jesus were on their way to Emmaus. The Gospel of John tells us that the risen Jesus also appeared to the disciples by the Sea of Tiberius, Matthew tells us that He appeared on a mountain in Galilee, and Luke tells us that He appeared on Mount Olivet just before His ascension. In the book of Acts, Luke tells us that Jesus presented Himself alive by many proofs, appearing to them during a forty-day period of time before He ascended into heaven. The point is that the so-called "proof" of the resurrection is not the *absence* of Jesus's body from the tomb, but the *presence* of the risen Jesus to His followers.

It was difficult to believe that Jesus was raised from the dead — but if you think about it, it is just as difficult to believe that Jesus would return to the very same ragtag group of followers who so disappointed Him, misunderstood Him, forsook Him, and fled into the darkness. He returned to the very people who had let Him down when He needed them the most.

Will Willimon wrote that some of us might have thought that the first day of His resurrected life, the risen Christ might have made His way straight to the palace, the seat of Roman power and appear to

Pontius Pilate, who had allowed Jesus to be condemned to death. We might have thought that the first day of His resurrected life, Jesus would have wanted to do something big to get maximum results and publicity. We might have thought that the risen Jesus would not have wasted His time talking to the first person He met on the street, but would have found a way to appear before the movers and shakers in Jerusalem, the influential and the powerful, those who had prestige and authority. But instead, Jesus went to Galilee. But why Galilee, of all places? Nobody special would be in Galilee … except His followers.

That first Easter, nobody actually saw Jesus rise from the dead. They saw Him afterwards. *They* did not appear to *Him*; *He* appeared to *them*. He came looking for them. In recounting and summarizing those post-resurrection appearances to the Corinthians, Paul began by listing the people to whom the risen Christ appeared in those first forty days after Easter. But Paul did not stop there. He went on to write those words that transform the Easter story from a third-person story to a first-person story: "He appeared also to *me*," Paul said. Some four or five years after all of these other post-resurrection appearances that we usually read about on Easter morning, some four or five years after the ascension of Jesus, and after all the dust had settled, the risen Jesus showed up again — this time to the great persecutor and murderer of the church we now know as Paul. It is clear that Paul was not seeking Jesus at all on the road to Damascus. In fact, Paul was seeking to snuff out this movement by making Jesus nothing more than a bloody memory of His misguided followers. But then Jesus appeared also to him, and nothing was ever the same again.

What makes the gospel such good news is not just that Jesus lived, but that Jesus lived *for us*. It is not just that Jesus died, but that Jesus died *for us*. And it is not just that Jesus was raised, but that Jesus was raised *for us*. And to prove that truth to us, His first order of business on Easter morning was to come looking for us and find us — not just during that forty-day window of time between His resurrection and His ascension, but still all these years later, He appears to us also. As He did to the disciples who failed Him, and to Saul who persecuted the church, He does to us. He comes looking for *us*. The risen Jesus appears also to *us*.

We might have thought when we walked away from the cross in silence and darkness on Friday night that it was over between us and God. At last, we had gone too far away. We had denied Him, betrayed Him, and forsaken Him and fled. We had stooped to the lowest low when we tortured God's own Son and nailed Him to a tree. But then on this Easter morning, He came back. And He came back to the very ones who had let Him down. He came back to *us*.

A professor once gave an assignment to his divinity school students to summarize the gospel in a few words, and one of his students wrote, "In the Bible, it gets dark, then it gets very, very, dark, then Jesus shows up." And the good news of Easter is that Jesus doesn't just show up. He shows up *for us*."[40]

To the poor, struggling Corinthians, failing at being the church, backsliding, wandering, split apart, faithless, scandalously immoral, Paul preached Easter in first person, saying to them and to us all, "He appeared also to me." He appeared even to me. For I am the least of the apostles," Paul wrote, "because I *persecuted* the church of God. But by the grace of God, I am what I am, and His grace toward me was not in vain."

That's the Easter story that continues by the sheer grace of God. That's what the risen Savior does. He comes back — again and again to the very ones (I'm talking about us!) who so betray and disappoint Him. He appears also to us, seeks us, finds us, embraces us, holds on to us, and then commissions us to do His work. The risen Christ is still at

---

[40] Willimon, 251.

work. He is on the loose, and will appear where you live, maybe even when and where you least expect Him.

Later in this same chapter, Paul argued that everything hinges on the resurrection. If Jesus had not appeared to those first disciples, their preaching would have been in vain. If Christ had not been raised, Paul said our faith would be in vain. If there were no resurrection, we would still be in our sins, and those who have died would have died without hope. "But," as Paul wrote, "in fact, Christ has been raised from the dead." And the way Paul could speak with such confidence was not just because of the tradition that had been passed along to him in third person, but because that third-person story had become a first-person reality. "He appeared also to me."

And I would add, "He has appeared also to *me*." As the man on his deathbed told his pastor, "I look back over my life, all the mistakes I've made, all the times I've turned away from Jesus, gone my own way, strayed, and got lost. And time and again, He found a way to get to me, showed up and got me, looked for me when I wasn't looking for Him." Even though we, like Paul, have never seen the risen Jesus in Person, He still appears to us. And for all I know, the risen Christ may be looking for you now, or looking for you again. And nothing would please Him more than for you to be able to say boldly to others what Paul said boldly to the Corinthians: "He appeared also to me … By the grace of God, I am what I am, and His grace toward me was not in vain."

In the Baptist tradition, we often sing a hymn that asks and answers the question, "How do we know Jesus lives?" And in the joyful refrain, the answer comes. We know He lives because we have the inward assurance that He lives within our hearts.[41]

---

41 Alfred H. Ackley. *Celebrating Grace* (Macon, Georgia: Celebrating Grace, Inc., 2010), 622.

He appeared also to me. The only way I can really know that the Easter story is true is because, by God's grace, the risen Jesus appeared also to me. And I am determined that His grace toward me will not be in vain.

The Motherly Love of God
A Mother's Day Sermon

ISAIAH 66:12-13

> ¹² *For thus says the Lord:*
> *I will extend prosperity to her like a river,*
> *and the wealth of the nations like an overflowing stream;*
> *and you shall nurse and be carried on her arm,*
> *and dandled on her knees.*
> ¹³ *As a mother comforts her child,*
> *so I will comfort you;*
> *you shall be comforted in Jerusalem.*

Do you remember the times when, as a child, you ran to your mother (or your mother figure) whenever you skinned your knee or scraped your arm? If your mother was like my mother, she was usually not too far away. It seemed she had a sixth sense, a way of knowing where you were and what you were doing at all times. Sometimes you might have gone to your father if you couldn't find your mother, or in some cases, maybe only your mother was around. But you would find your mother and crawl up in her lap. She would kiss the hurt, and it would go away. Have you ever wondered what was really going on in that transaction? Exactly how did that happen? How did the hurt go away? Was there medicinal value in your mother's kiss? Was it magical? And have you ever figured out why no one else's kiss would work the same way?

By far, the most dominant parental image of God in the Bible is the image of God as Father. But, tucked away in the back corner of Isaiah's prophecy, in one of the tenderest passages in all of Scripture, the prophet holds before us a radical, albeit brief, glimpse of God not as a Father, but as a Mother. Of course, all the human analogies and metaphors the Bible uses for God break down at a certain point. God is Spirit, and is always beyond anything even the Bible says. But each analogy the Bible gives us reveals something more of God's nature and character. And that is why the Bible most often uses the parent-child relationship to describe our relationship with God. The point of the comparison is not so much the gender of God, but the parenthood of God. The best and clearest way for us to understand how God relates to us and how we are to relate to God is the parent-child analogy. And that is because all of us are either parents or have been parented. We all know what it is to have parental figures in our lives. And whether we had good parents, bad parents, or no parents at all, we all long for the nurturing that only a parent figure can give us. So most often, the Bible pictures God as Father — but on this Mother's Day, we focus on this passage in which God is pictured as a Mother.

If it is true now, it was even truer then that the Father was regarded as the disciplinarian in the family, and I can certainly relate to that. My father was quite the disciplinarian, although my mother could be surprisingly firm when she needed to. In some families, the father is the one who punishes. In healthy families, the father disciplines appropriately but firmly not because he does not care about his children, but because he *does* care about them. He disciplines and punishes them because he loves them, and even his judgments are expressions of his deep and abiding love. In some families, not all, all the mother has to say to her children is, "You just wait till your daddy gets home." That line used to put the fear of God in me, and I can't count the number of times my mother used that line. Actually, we got it twice. My mother would punish us first; then when Daddy came home, he finished the job in his own special way.

Depending on your relationship with your father or lack of relationship, you may have some of those same associations in your mind about the role of the father in the family. I realize that I am painting with a broad stroke here. Not all fathers are disciplinarians, and not all mothers are tender. Some people have regrettable memories of abusive or neglectful parents, and any talk of God being like a Father or even a Mother is too painful to consider. But the Bible portrays God as the ideal Parent, a beautiful blend of qualities that many people in biblical times and in our own time associate with a father or a mother. In the historical and cultural context in which this passage was written, fathers tended to show their love by establishing the rules and enforcing them, and God knows that discipline is one of the most loving things any parent can do for his or her child. But children also need tenderness, compassion, and pity when they are hurt, and these qualities people in that time (and in our time, too) were more likely to associate with mothers. Sometimes single parents in our culture often face the challenge of acting as both a father and a mother, but it is rare for one person to possess the right balance of discipline and mercy. Most of us, as parents and as human beings, tend to err on one side or the other. And if our children are fortunate, there will be some other parental figure in their lives to bring balance. The truth is that we all need the right balance of both discipline and mercy. That's just the way we were made.

The people of God had had their share of discipline. It is true that they deserved everything they got. They had it coming to them. And they had been warned over and over again by the prophets. But when the discipline came, it was swift and severe, and they were devastated. The setting of this passage in Isaiah is the aftermath of the Babylonian exile, when God's people were invited to come back home after a long time away. But if you have ever been away from home for any length of time and have come back, you realize it's not the same as it was when you left. That was especially true when the exiled people made their way back to their home land. The Babylonian army had left it in shambles. The temple would have to be re-built one stone at a time. It appeared they had no good options. For that reason, some decided to stay in Babylon — but others decided that they would go back home and begin the tedious work of putting their shattered lives back together again.

My former pastor, Ansel McGill, used to say, "Sometimes we are judged not so much *for* our sins, but *by* our sins." There were severe consequences for the sins of God's people. And, like a parent, God knows that sometimes the only way for children to learn the lessons of life is the hard way. God did not have to bring on the discipline. They had brought it on themselves.

But the Bible doesn't stop there. It never does. God is not just a God of discipline, but also a God of grace. The same God who punishes out of love also shows mercy out of the same love. The exile was not the end of the story. When the children of God came back home, the prophet promised that, like a mother, God would be there waiting to receive them with open arms. First, the prophet compares the land itself, the land of Judah, to a mother. But then, in a rare and bold moment of inspiration, he shows us that God, who is beyond any human analogy that even the Bible can offer, possesses qualities that can best be understood in motherly terms.

For thus says the Lord: "… As a mother comforts her child, so I will comfort you."

God is like a father who loves us enough to make rules and set boundaries for our own good. But God is also like a mother, who picks us up when we fall, who tenderly kisses away our pain, and hurts when we hurt. In the mother-father analogies, the dual nature of God is expressed. God is a God of discipline and mercy. And regardless of what parental images you may have grown up with, God's nature reveals the best traits of a good father and a good mother. In that sense, God is a single parent who acts as both father and mother to us.

For some of us, Mother's Day is a day filled with warm and beautiful memories. But for others of us, Mother's Day may bring up more pain than joy. Some of us know what it is to have a father and mother who love us. They may not have been perfect parents, but we grew up with a healthy, balanced understanding of parenthood. Certainly that was the case with me, and I am thankful. But not everyone is so blessed. Many of us did not have a positive role model for a father or mother, and it is harder to relate to God as a parent. But the Bible invites us to think of God as the perfect blend of fatherly and motherly love.

For thus says the Lord: "… As a mother comforts her child, so I will comfort you."

But all of this talk about God as our Parent implies that we are the children. And frankly, the problem for most of us is not so much that we refuse to see God as a parent. The problem for most of us is that we refuse to see ourselves as the children. It is beneath many of us to think of ourselves as dependent children. We prefer to think of ourselves as independent and self-sufficient. We have been conditioned by our culture not to admit our weaknesses, and to cover up our vulnerabilities. Often our bravado is only a cover. We do not know nearly as much as we think we do. We do not have the power we wish we did. We are often too proud to admit our failures and sins. But what most of us need more than anything else is to crawl up again in our Mother's lap and let Her kiss away our hurts. Jesus reminded us that, if we think we are too big to come to God as children, then we are too big to come to God at all (Matthew 18:3).

Knowing this sermon was coming, I thought about that a couple of weeks ago. I had begun to realize that I was in over my head. I was letting the pressure of life get to me, and I was feeling like such a failure in almost every way. Life was hard, and I was down for the count. And I found myself making my way back to 23 Harrington Avenue, where I grew up and where I have returned many times since I left home. When I split my chin open on the fence I was not supposed to climb, I ran home. When I was injured playing baseball or basketball, I ran home. When I was sick, I just wanted to be home. When I learned to drive and had to find my way around, I always had to start at 23 Harrington Avenue before I could get to where I was going. The place itself was and still is sacred to me.

But eventually I realized that home is not finally about a place, but about a person. Even though I am a parent myself, when life gets hard, I still find my way back to 23 Harrington Avenue. And I still feel like, if I can just get there, everything will be all right — because there, in that place I have learned to call home, I have a mother who will love me no matter what, who will heal my deepest hurt, and can still take my hurts away — not necessarily by saying anything memorable or doing anything magical, but just by being who she is and inspiring me to be all I can be. I didn't crawl up in my mother's lap that day (for fear that I would crush her), but I did stretch out in the empty recliner beside hers and pour out my heart to her. And as I did, my hurt became more bearable. She didn't fix my situation — but she fixed me. She helped me put it all in perspective. She did what mothers do best. She loved me and she comforted me as only a mother can. What makes her love so special and her comfort so effective is that I belong to her. I literally came from her. I am a part of her, and she is a part of me. So when I hurt, she hurts. And no matter how big I get, or how big I think I am, I will never outgrow her love for me. No matter how old she gets and no matter how old I get, she will never quit being my mother, and I will never quit being her child.

That is the picture of God here in this passage. After a long exile, the children of God found their way back home to the land that was sacred to them. And when they got there, they realized that the words of the prophet were no longer just a dream, but a reality. God had given birth to them. They belonged to God and God belonged to them. They were a part of God and God was a part of them. In the beginning, they came from God — and now as they were beginning again, they came back to God, who, like a good mother, was there to welcome them home and heal their broken hearts.

And that is what God will do for you today. Whatever we are going through, however far away from home we may be, God is like a good mother who will welcome us home. Like a good mother, God hurts when we hurt, even when we deserve to hurt. And that is because we belong to God. We came from God. And when we drop the pretense and come to God as little children, the promise of Scripture will become a reality, and the motherly love of God will heal our broken hearts. **As a mother comforts her children, so God will comfort us.** Amen.

Outloved by the Father

A Father's Day Sermon

LUKE 15:20-24

> [20] *So he set off and went to his father. But while he was still far off, his father saw him and was filled with compassion; he ran and put his arms around him and kissed him.* [21] *Then the son said to him, "Father, I have sinned against heaven and before you; I am no longer worthy to be called your son."* [22] *But the father said to his slaves, "Quickly, bring out a robe — the best one — and put it on him; put a ring on his finger and sandals on his feet.* [23] *And get the fatted calf and kill it, and let us eat and celebrate;* [24] *for this son of mine was dead and is alive again; he was lost and is found!" And they began to celebrate.*

Today is my first Father's Day without my father. Last year on Father's Day, I preached about "The Greatest Words Never Spoken" and talked about the importance of saying "I love you" to the people we love the most. My father was never one to throw those words around too often. "It's understood," he used to say. "Anybody can say it," he would add — to which we would reply, "Well, apparently not. You can't say it." But last year, it was different. After lunch, he went around the room and told each one of us individually that he loved us. We had no way of knowing (but looking back I wonder if somehow he knew) that would be his last Father's Day with us. Just two months later, he died.

Today our family will gather at our house for lunch — and there will be an empty place around the table, and an even bigger empty place in our hearts. We don't plan it this way, but every time we get together now, we quote Daddy and keep his memory alive by remembering some of his famous sayings, some of which I will not repeat here. One of the things he used to say often was, "You will never mean as much to your children as your children mean to you."

I have thought often about that quote, especially this week as I re-read the story we now call "The Prodigal Son." I have always thought that story was mis-named. More than a story about the escapades of a wasteful and irresponsible son, this story is about the grace and extravagance of a loving father. Most of us know the story about the younger son who could not even wait for his father to die before he asked for his share of the inheritance. The father, knowing the son was about to make a big mistake, gave the son what he asked for, and his son went as far away from home as he could go and wasted his inheritance. But soon he ran out of money and options, and bottomed out in a pigpen. He had partied out, only to realize that the real party was at home with the father. He didn't have to leave home to find what he really needed. He had to lose what he could not keep before he could re-gain what he could not lose.

So he came to himself and to his senses and made his way back home, preparing to beg if need be. He was giving up on ever being treated as a son again. He was just going to ask to be treated like one of the servants. All the way home, he rehearsed his speech, "Father, I have sinned against heaven and before you; I am no longer worthy to be called your son; treat me as one of your hired servants." And he made his way back home.

Meanwhile, back at home, the father was waiting. One of the hardest things a parent can do is to let our children go and wait until they come to their senses and make their way back home. The father kept the porch light on. The entire time the younger son was away, he kept the home fires burning … waiting and longing and loving. And it was the power of that love that compelled the son to come home.

One day, the father was out on the porch like he always was, still on the lookout for his wandering son, when in the far distance, he saw his son coming home. He couldn't wait for the son to get there, so he ran to meet his son, hugged him and kissed him and welcomed him home. Immediately, the son began to recite his rehearsed speech, but the father would not hear it. He interrupted the son, called for the servants to bring the best robe and put it on him, a ring for his finger, and shoes for his feet. Then the father threw a party in honor of his son.

The son lived long enough to learn to appreciate his father. He grew to love his father and to realize the value of what his father had done for him. He could come back home and beg for forgiveness. He could come back home and try the rest of his days to please his father. He could try to make up for lost time and missed opportunities. He could love his father the best way he knew how. But one thing he could never do. He could never outlove his father.

I used to read a book to my girls at bedtime called *Guess How Much I Love You*.[42] It was about a daddy rabbit and a baby rabbit who had this conversation about how much they loved each other. The little rabbit stretched out his arms as wide as they could go, and said, "I love you this much."

But Big Nutbrown Hare had even longer arms. And as he stretched out his arms as wide as they could go, he said, "But I love *you* this much." As the book goes on, the baby rabbit keeps trying to show the daddy

---

42 Sam McBratney. *Guess How Much I Love You* (Cambridge, Massachusetts: Candlewick Press).

rabbit how much he loves him. But the daddy rabbit's arms were always longer and wider.

I thought about that this week as I remembered my own father, specifically the last night of his life. It was my turn to spend the night with him in the hospital. It was dark, and it was stormy. He was having trouble getting comfortable, and nothing I did seemed to help. And finally, he said, "Just take my hand." And as I held his hand in the darkness and heard the thunder and rain, I quoted my daddy's favorite Bible verse and sang his favorite hymn. In that moment, I remember thinking how much I loved him. And then I remembered what he told me. "You will never mean as much to your children as your children mean to you." Looking back on it, I realize now that was Daddy's way of saying in death what was so hard for him to say in life: "No matter how much you love me, I love you more."

And so today, no matter where you are or what you've done, you have a Father who loves you more than you could ever love him. No matter how far away from home you may be, your Father's arms are open wide. And no matter how much you love Him, He loves you more. Amen.

The Intersection of God and Country

An Independence Day Sermon

MARK 12:13-17

> ¹³ Then they sent to him some Pharisees and some Herodians to trap him in what he said. ¹⁴ And they came and said to him, "Teacher, we know that you are sincere, and show deference to no one; for you do not regard people with partiality, but teach the way of God in accordance with truth. Is it lawful to pay taxes to the emperor, or not? ¹⁵ Should we pay them, or should we not?" But knowing their hypocrisy, he said to them, "Why are you putting me to the test? Bring me a denarius and let me see it." ¹⁶ And they brought one. Then he said to them, "Whose head is this, and whose title?" They answered, "The emperor's." ¹⁷ Jesus said to them, "Give to the emperor the things that are the emperor's, and to God the things that are God's." And they were utterly amazed at him.

Ask Jesus a simple question, and you almost never get a simple answer. And when you *do* get an answer, it's usually not the answer you want. It's certainly not that Jesus didn't *know* the answers; it is that Jesus realized that there is often more value added by asking the right question than by giving the right answer. That is just another way of saying that Jesus often caused more confusion that He settled. So if you are coming to Jesus hoping He will resolve your confusion, you might be disappointed. It appears that Jesus knew that we have to feel the confusion before we can ever hope to gain clarity, which is why He raised as many questions as He ever answered, and why He was content to leave some questions open and unanswered. At every turn, He resisted the temptation to reduce the Christian faith to an official set of answers — and that was never more the case than when the confusion was around the intersection of faith and politics.

Jesus's presence, His teachings, and His very life caused people to ask questions. And rather than giving the answers, which presumably He could have done, He most often chose to intensify the questions and then leave the questioners to deal with their questions in a different light. He did not spoon-feed His followers and do their thinking for them. He did not tell them *what* to think, but he showed them *how* to think. Rather than ending their search, Jesus helped His questioners see that their search was just beginning. Sometimes, the questioners would find Jesus's responses exciting and stimulating. Sometimes, Jesus told people more than they wanted to know. And sometimes, people went away wishing they had never asked. But you ask Jesus a simple question, and you almost never get a simple answer.

Consider, for example, the curious alliance between religion and politics that was formed in this passage of Scripture from Mark's Gospel. The Pharisees were a religious group totally devoted to the Torah and the oral traditions that developed around the Hebrew Scriptures and the Jewish faith. They were passionately religious. The Herodians were a political party that attached itself to the dynasty of Herod. They had been replaced by Roman governors and wanted the return of the Herodian dynasty to Judea. It is a fascinating alliance for many reasons — not the least of which is that it shows how faith and politics have a long history of forming unholy alliances. In this case, the Pharisees and the

Herodians joined forces against Jesus, whom both groups considered to be their adversary. Of course, their alliance was one of convenience, and their sole purpose was to get rid of Jesus, whom they considered to be a threat to their respective agendas.

But, in order to prove that idea, they first had to gather evidence that Jesus was a threat to the political stability of that region. And their plan was to use the issue of taxation to entrap Jesus. The Roman tax system invited corruption at every level of the government from Caesar himself to the local tax collectors, who were despised and presumed to be dishonest and corrupt. The issue of taxation has always been a hot-button issue, and tax collectors have never been at the top of the list of reputable occupations. And really, the issue is not just about money in particular, but about control in general. What is and what should be the role of government in the ordering of our national and political life together?

That question is one of the primary fault lines between the two major political parties in our country today. Some people believe that the government should have almost no role in our lives (or at least a very minimal role) — and some people believe that the government should have more of proactive and expansive role in our lives, ordering our life together. But most of us live somewhere in the middle of the two extremes. We want to pay taxes, but not too much taxes. We want the government to exert control, but not too much control. We enjoy some of the services we support with our tax dollars, but we strongly object to some of the initiatives our tax dollars support. So what are we to do? How should we vote? What should we support and what should we oppose? And when you introduce faith into the mix, the questions surrounding government control and taxation become even more complicated.

The Pharisees and Herodians had already decided that Jesus had to go, but they needed the political support of the government, so they formed an alliance to entrap Jesus in a conversation about taxation and the role of government. At this point in their planning, trapping Jesus in *religious* heresy would not be enough; He must be trapped in remarks that would constitute political treason, giving His accusers grounds to bring Him before the governor, Pontius Pilate. Listen to the way they tried to bait Jesus with flattering words, but hostile intent: "Teacher, we know that you are sincere, and show deference to no one; for you do not regard people with partiality, but teach the way of God in accordance with truth. Is it lawful to pay taxes to the emperor, or not?" (Mark 12:14). But Mark tells us that Jesus saw right through their flattering masquerade and just let them continue. In an atmosphere of anti-Roman revolts, they asked, "Is it lawful for us to give tribute to Caesar, or not?" It was their way of trying to get Jesus to declare Himself one way or the other. If Jesus had said yes, then He would have been supporting a corrupt and oppressive tax system. If He had said no, then He would have been fanning the flames of a revolt and rebellion against the Roman government. It would be about like our asking Jesus, "Are you a Republican or a Democrat? Do you want higher taxes or lower taxes? Do you think the government should have a major role in our lives or a minor role in our lives? Because whatever You say, we know that You represent and teach the way of God." It is the oldest trick in the book to try to co-opt God and get God on our side. It seems like a simple question: "Is it lawful to pay taxes to Caesar or not?" But if you ask Jesus a simple question, you almost never get a simple answer.

Knowing their hypocrisy, Jesus asked, "Why are you putting me to the test? You got a coin on you?" (my paraphrase of Mark 12:15). It is worth noting that Jesus didn't have a coin of His own. Someone brought Him a coin, and then Jesus asked, "Whose head is this? And whose title?" (Mark 12:16) — answering their question with a question of His own.

"The emperor's," they said (Mark 12:16). The answer was obvious.

Then Jesus took control of the conversation and said, "Then give to the emperor the things that are the emperor's, and to God, the things that are God's" (Mark 12:17). And I know they must have been thinking, "Okay, so it is lawful for us to give tribute to Caesar, or not?" And Mark tells us that these religious and political representatives were utterly amazed (Mark 12:17). Somehow, in the course of that brief conversation, Jesus had turned the question back on them and left them speechless.

Some interpreters have concluded that, by referring to Caesar's image on the coin, Jesus was teaching that, of course, the government has a rightful claim on our money. Of course, it is lawful to pay taxes to the government. But other interpreters have said, "Not so fast." By asking what belongs to God, Jesus was implying that God has a rightful claim over everything — not just our money — and that *God's* claim upon our lives supersedes any authority that the government may have.

This time is as good as any to recognize the tension that often exists between our loyalty to God and our loyalty to country. Every Sunday, when many Christians gather for worship, they find themselves worshiping between two flags: the Christian flag and the American flag. As a child, I grew up pledging allegiance to both flags in Vacation Bible School. But it was not until I became much older that I realized what tension there is when we pledge allegiance to more than one flag. So we are left with an open question that Jesus *didn't* answer and His questioners *couldn't* answer: What belongs to Caesar? And what belongs to God?

Sometimes confusion and conflictedness can be productive emotions, especially if those emotions are informed by Jesus and cause us to think again about what and who belongs to God. Any time we are confused and conflicted about situations in our lives, there is an opportunity for us to reaffirm where and how God fits into the situations of our lives. And that is especially true in regards to the intersection of faith and politics, God and country.

Jesus did us a great service by intensifying our confusion, by taking the question that was posed to Him, which is an important question, and turning it into an infinitely more important question.

So what is the role of government in our lives as individuals and in our life together as a nation? Some argue for a limited role and lower taxes, and some argue for a more expansive role and higher taxes. And all of us have to decide in our personal lives, in our political philosophy, and at the ballot box what it means to be a patriotic, responsible citizen of this country. How do we render unto Caesar the things that are Caesar's? It is an open question that Jesus refused to answer.

I aways assume that I am preaching to a bunch of party loyalists who have decided that the truth lies in the positions of one or the other political party. But I believe Jesus left some questions open intentionally — not to resolve our confusion, but to intensify it, until the confusion produces a better result than an easy, knee-jerk answer ever would have. If the questions that Jesus left open are ever closed, and the debate ever stops, then the freedoms we enjoy and celebrate in this country will be lost in the exchange. That is why on some issues, I would much rather have thoughtful confusion than false certainty.

What we give to Caesar is an important question to consider and debate. But Jesus shifted the conversation from that question to another question that is infinitely more important and relevant to who we are as a church. What belongs to God? It is not an overstatement to say that eternity hinges on some form of that question. This question is bigger than whether we should pay taxes or not. It is bigger than what political party we support. It is bigger than who will be our governor or even who will be our President. This question is about who will be our Lord.

And the way we answer that question will inform us as we struggle with all the confusion and conflictedness of our lives. While taxes still come due, we worship here every Sunday standing in the tension between these two flags, and make the confession that Jesus Christ is Lord. In the church, that is one question that is not open. So what does it mean to render to God the things that are God's? A biblical answer to that question is that all things belong to God. As Paul wrote in his letter to the Romans, "*From* Him and *through* Him and *to* Him are all things. To Him be glory forever" (Romans 11:36).

I love to hear and sing the patriotic music that sends chills down our spines and puts lumps in our throats. But in the church, before we read the Constitution, we read the Bible. Before we sing the songs of our country, we sing the songs of our faith. Before we sing *America, the Beautiful,* we sing *Jesus Is Lord of All.* While some confusion and conflictedness might be productive, we must never be confused about this: Everything we have belongs to God. And everything we are belongs to God. And everything we hope to be belongs to God. And before we ever pledge allegiance to the flag of any country, we pledge our ultimate loyalty to God and God alone, to whom be glory forever. Amen.

Some Blessings You May Not Have Counted

A Thanksgiving Sermon

LUKE 6:20-26

---

²⁰ *Then he looked up at his disciples and said:*

"Blessed are you who are poor,
for yours is the kingdom of God.
²¹ *"Blessed are you who are hungry now,*
for you will be filled.
"Blessed are you who weep now,
for you will laugh.

²² *"Blessed are you when people hate you, and when they exclude you, revile you, and defame you on account of the Son of Man.* ²³ *Rejoice in that day and leap for joy, for surely your reward is great in heaven; for that is what their ancestors did to the prophets.*

²⁴ *"But woe to you who are rich,*
for you have received your consolation.
²⁵ *"Woe to you who are full now,*
for you will be hungry.
"Woe to you who are laughing now,
for you will mourn and weep.

²⁶ *"Woe to you when all speak well of you, for that is what their ancestors did to the false prophets.*

At this time of year, it is customary for us to take the time to count our blessings. As the psalmist wrote, "It is good to give thanks to the LORD." We don't do it often enough, and we might not be doing it now if it we were not in the Thanksgiving season. As we begin to name our blessings one by one, many of us will list our wealth and material blessings. Before we eat the turkey and dressing, we will bow our heads and thank God that we have more than enough to eat. As we count our blessings, many of us will thank God for the gift of laughter, good times and pleasant memories. And some of us will thank God for the people in our lives who believe in us and think we are better than we know we really are. Not only do we feel blessed, but we feel good about being thankful for our blessings.

And so, in some ways, it seems like such a shame on an occasion like this, to read a passage like the one we read earlier from the Sermon on the Plain in Luke's Gospel. It's just like Jesus to mess up our Thanksgiving celebration, to keep us from feeling too good about our so-called "blessings." "I know what you think," Jesus said, "but the blessed ones are those who are poor, the ones who are hungry, the ones who are weeping, and the ones who are persecuted. And the ones who are to be pitied are those who are enjoying wealth, food, laughter, and esteem." I don't know about you, but poverty, hunger, tears, and hatred are some blessings that I would not have counted. If this is what it is to be blessed, then I would just as soon not be blessed. It's pretty bad when you can't even feel good on Thanksgiving.

But we shouldn't be surprised that Jesus would make us feel so displaced unsettled. We should have seen it coming early in Luke's story when Mary proclaimed before Jesus was even born, as if it had already happened, "He has put down the mighty from their thrones and exalted those of low degree. He has filled the hungry with good things, and

Some Blessings You May Not Have Counted

the rich he has sent empty away." The kingdom of God is a kingdom of surprises. Values are turned inside out and upside down. Insiders become outsiders, and the last become first.

I think sometimes it may be hard for us to get a sense of the original shock value of these words. Beatitudes were common and popular forms of speech. They were short, two-part affirmations that summed up commonly accepted, predictable sound bites of wisdom. "Blessed are they who attend community Thanksgiving services, for they shall feel good about themselves" — that sort of thing. So the *form* of what Jesus said was familiar. But the *substance* was unpredictable and disturbing. Instead of following the expected line of thought and presenting commonly accepted nuggets of wisdom that no one would have questioned, Jesus re-defined what it means to be blessed. Surprisingly, he equated blessedness with the very things that most of us try hard to avoid: poverty, hunger, grief, and hatred. I don't usually count those experiences as blessings, and I doubt if you do either.

And each beatitude has a mirror image in the Sermon on the Plain, which only Luke seemed to know about. These woes were pronounced against the people who had the very things that most people try to achieve: wealth, food, laughter, and esteem. In other words, the very blessings we may have counted may not be blessings at all, or if they are, they are, at best mixed blessings. By the time Jesus got through talking, the bad things sounded good and the good things sounded bad. As Dr. Melton used to tell us in New Testament class, "The problem with most of us is not that we are empty and need to be filled; it is that we are filled and need to be emptied."

An investment banker was at the pier of a small coastal village when a small boat with just one fisherman docked. Inside the small boat were several large yellow fin tuna. The banker complimented the fisherman on the quality of his fish and asked how long it took to catch them. The fisherman replied, "Only a little while."

The banker then asked why didn't he stay out longer and catch more fish? The fisherman said he had enough to support his family's immediate needs. The banker then asked, "But what do you do with the rest of your time?"

The fisherman said, "I sleep late, fish a little, play with my children, take a nap with my wife, stroll into the village each evening where I play guitar and sing with my friends. I have a full and busy life."

The banker scoffed, "I am a Harvard MBA and I could help you. You should spend more time fishing and with the proceeds, buy a bigger boat. With the proceeds from the bigger boat, you could buy several boats, eventually you would have a fleet of fishing boats. Instead of selling your catch to a middleman, you would sell directly to the processor, eventually opening your own cannery. You would control the product, processing and distribution. You would need to leave this small coastal fishing village and move to a big city where you will run your expanding enterprise."

The fisherman asked, "But, how long will this all take?" to which the banker replied, "Fifteen to twenty years."

"But what then?"

The banker laughed and said that's the best part. "When the time is right, you would announce an IPO and sell your company stock to the public and become very rich. You would make millions."

"Millions? Then what?"

The banker said, "Then you would retire. Move to a small coastal fishing village where you would sleep late, fish a little, play with your kids, take a nap with your wife, stroll to the village in the evenings where you could play your guitar and sing with your friends."[43]

---

43 Tony Evans. *Tony Evans' Book of Illustrations: Stories, Quotes and Anecdotes* (Chicago: Moody Press, 2009), 346-347.

Sometimes in spite of how it may seem, the people who have the least have the most. Sometimes the very blessings we are seeking are right before our very eyes.

And yet, these beatitudes do not come to us in the form of advice. Jesus was not commanding anybody to do anything. We automatically assume that the blessings must be what He wants us to seek and the woe things must be what He wants us to avoid. But that is not the point. It is not that Jesus wants you to quit work and become poor, or quit eating and become hungry, or try to find some reason to stop laughing and start crying, or do your best to ruin your reputation so no one will speak well of you — just so that you can move from one list to the other.

The beatitudes do not tell us what to do. They tell us who we are. And more importantly, they tell us who Jesus is. Jesus never said who was who. He just described different kinds of people, so that His listeners might recognize themselves as one kind or another, and He makes the same promise to them all: that the way things are now is not the way they will always be. Barbara Brown Taylor likens this passage to a Ferris wheel that goes around, up and down, so that those who are at the top will have their turn at the bottom, while those who are down there right now will have their chance to make their way to the top. This is the truth about how life works, spoken by One who loves everyone on that wheel. But how you hear these words is definitely determined by who you are and where you are right now.[44]

For some of us, the Thanksgiving season brings more sorrow than joy. When some of us count our blessings, and name them one by one, our list seems too short. Thanksgiving can be a joyful reminder of what we *do* have, but it can also be a painful reminder of what we do *not* have.

---

44 Barbara Brown Taylor. *Home by Another Way* (Boston: Cowley Publications, 1999), 55.

And where you are on the Ferris wheel has everything to do with how you take these words.

Jesus said:

> "Blessed are you who are poor, for you already know what it is to be dependent upon God. Blessed are you who are hungry now, for there will come a day when you will be filled. Blessed are you who weep now, for you may not have anything to laugh about now, but you will. Blessed are you when people hate you, and when they exclude you, revile you, and defame you on my account. That is actually a good thing for two reasons: your reward in heaven will be great, and you are in good company because that is what people did to the prophets before you.
>
> "But woe to you who are rich, for you may be enjoying your wealth now, but wealth carries with it no lasting value. Woe to you who are full now, for eventually you will know what it is to be empty. Woe to you who are laughing now, for the day will come when you will mourn and weep. Woe to you when all speak well of you, for that does not mean you are as good as they all seem to think you are. Don't feel too good about yourself because people used to speak well of the false prophets, too."

So ... happy Thanksgiving! This passage does not tell us what to do, but it does tell us who we are. And depending on where we find ourselves on the Ferris wheel, we may have more or fewer blessings to count than we may have thought. For sometimes blessedness comes to us in the most painful and unexpected forms.

An unknown confederate soldier asked for God's blessings and left this conclusion behind:

> I asked God for strength, that I might achieve;
> I was made weak that I might learn humbly to obey.
> I asked for help that I might do greater things;
> I was given infirmity, that I might do better things.
> I asked for riches, that I might be happy;
> I was given poverty that I might be wise.
> I asked for power that I might have the praise of men;
> I was given weakness that I might feel the need of God.
> I asked for all things that I might enjoy my life;
> I was given life that I might enjoy all things.
> I got nothing I asked for, but everything I had hoped for.
> I am among men most richly blessed.[45]

So this Thanksgiving season, we might want to think twice before we ask God to bless us. God may just do it.

---

45 Thomas C. Oden. *Pastoral Theology: Essentials of Ministry* (New York: Harper and Row Publishers, Inc., 1983), 248.

Epilogue

Preachers never preach alone. There are always people who stand behind them, beside them, and before them.

Behind preachers are all the people who influenced them. In my case, the most formative influences were my parents, who influenced my preaching without even realizing it. In my previous book, *23: Growing Up in the Space between Harry and Celeste*, I tried to summarize the ways my parents shaped my personality and eventually my ministry. I am so aware that, behind almost all of my sermons is the influence of my parents: my father's honest and humorous approach to matters of faith, and my mother's pure heart and genuine trust in Jesus.

Also behind me are teachers and professors who molded me and shaped me into the preacher that I am. In my case, there were three professors at Furman University who taught me how to think about the truth of Scripture. Robert Crapps, who literally wrote the textbook we used in the Old Testament Survey class that he taught, made me think for the first time about the truth of the Old Testament from a historical, literary, and critical point of view. Joe King, my Church History Professor, helped me understand that my theology was not just shaped by the Bible, but by the historical interpretations and debates of the Church through the centuries. Theron Price, my Theology Professor, helped me clarify not just what I believed, but why I believed it. While I was a student at Furman, I was serving on staff part-time at Pelham Road Baptist Church, gaining practical church experience, but not sure about the direction my vocation would take me. Even though I majored in Economics and Business Administration, I realize now that there was a reason why, by my senior year, I was taking only the required courses for my major, and all the electives I could in the Religion Department. When I graduated from Furman, I got a job not in a business, but in a church that graciously gave me a place to determine my vocational path. Not long after I started serving Calvary Baptist Church, I was sure that God was leading me into a church-related vocation.

Three years passed between the time I graduated from Furman (1981) and the time I entered Erskine Theological Seminary (1984), and I was unprepared for the profound ways my experience at Erskine would mold me as a person, a follower of Jesus, and a minister. All of my professors took a personal interest in all their students. They spent time with me before and after class. In some cases, they invited me to their homes or to have lunch or dinner with them. I learned as much from them outside the classroom as I did inside the classroom. Some seminaries and divinity schools (on the right and on the left of the theological spectrum) indoctrinate students, teaching them what to think. But my experience in seminary was the same as my experience at Furman: My professors taught us how to think. They introduced us to a spectrum of views in mainstream Christianity, expected us to be familiar and conversant with those views, and then encouraged us to be thoughtful and intentional about where on that spectrum we would identify our own views. At that time, students at Erskine were not just Presbyterians (ARP, PCUSA, and PCA), but Baptists, Methodists. African Methodist Episcopal, Church of God, Assembly of God, Lutherans, and even a few Catholics and Episcopalians. The racial, cultural, theological, and denominational diversity at Erskine in the 1980s was one of Erskine's most appealing qualities. It was so helpful for a white, lifelong Southern Baptist from a wonderful, but homogenous, home church to be exposed to students and professors who did

Epilogue

not always see the Bible or the Christian faith in the same way I did.

Many of my professors at Erskine are now deceased, and only one of them is still teaching at Erskine. Randy Ruble was the Vice President and Dean of the Seminary. He was the one who welcomed me into his office as a prospective student. When I left his office that day, I knew that Erskine was the place for me. Dr. Ruble also taught me Supervised Ministry. David Van Gelder taught me pastoral care and counseling; Robert Claytor, Supervised Clinical Experience; Joseph Gettys and Mary-Ruth Marshall, Christian Education; Bob Hall, Worship and Preaching; Bill Kuykendall, Hebrew and Old Testament; John Carson, Theology and Ethics; Ray King, Church History and Baptist History; Merwyn Johnson, Theology and Hermeneutics, and also the Director of the Doctor of Ministry program. There is no way to measure the magnitude of their influence on me. Even though some of them are no longer with us in this life, and I have lost contact with some of them who have retired, they all stand behind me every time I preach.

The one Erskine professor who is still teaching at Erskine molded me in the most profound ways, and continues to enrich my life. Loyd Melton taught me Greek and New Testament, Church Administration, Christian Mission, and other electives. He was the Chair of my Doctor of Ministry Committee, and was responsible for my being chosen as an adjunct professor at Erskine for seventeen years. I have asked him to teach and preach in several of the churches I have served, and am honored not only to call him my professor, but also my friend. He never taught me everything he knew, but sometimes it seems as though he taught me everything I ever knew about the Greek language as well as the history and literature of the New Testament. He stands behind me every time I preach.

But so do all the pastors with whom I have had the privilege to serve. In one way or another, they were all mentors to me during different phases of my spiritual journey. Gerald Roper was the pastor of my home church (Central Baptist Church) when I graduated from Furman and was trying to decide what to do with my life. He helped me put together my first résumé and network with other pastors and denominational representatives who were in a position to support and encourage me. Bill Marler was the pastor who first gave me a chance to get my feet wet in church-related ministry, first at Pelham Road Baptist Church (my first part-time church staff experience) and then at Calvary Baptist Church (my first full-time church staff experience). Bill was the one who helped me clarify my call into ministry and my need for seminary training. Joe Roberts, longtime Assistant to the President of Furman University, was my interim pastor three times in two churches: Central Baptist once and Pelham Road Baptist twice. Ansel McGill was the longtime pastor of Parisview Baptist Church. I learned so much from Ansel about what it means to please God first, and others second. Ron Grizzle was the pastor of First Baptist Church in Simpsonville. If it had not been for Ron's support when I was going through the darkest time of my life, I am sure I would not have survived in ministry. Marshall Sargent was the longtime pastor of Eastlan Baptist Church. He had been my good friend for many years, and we never dreamed that we would ever have the opportunity to work together. But in the providence of God, we did. Jim Wooten was the longtime pastor of Earle Street Baptist Church. I served for seven years as associate pastor with Jim — and because of his influence, I was given the opportunity to serve as senior pastor of Earle Street when Jim resigned to become the senior pastor of The Baptist Church of Beaufort. All of these pastors became more than just mentors to me. They were friends to me — and every time I stand to preach, they stand behind me.

And then there are other preachers whose books of sermons have informed and inspired me. Not only have I benefited from these preachers' published sermons, but I have had the privilege of hearing and meeting them as well: Tom Long, Barbara Brown Taylor, Fred Craddock, Will Willimon, and Chuck Poole. It is not that I agree with everything they have said or written, but their biblical insights and illustrations have given me rich sermon material. I try to give them credit every time I quote them in a sermon (which is often), but even when I do not quote or refer to them directly, their preaching is always in the background of mine. They don't know it, but every time I stand to preach, they stand behind me.

Then there is the one who stands beside me when I preach — not literally — but when I preach, she may as well be standing beside me. During the week, she frees me up to prepare, work, and study. She gives me space to think and pray and be quiet. As a mother, she understands that preaching is about labor and delivery — and once the sermon has been delivered, the preacher is exhausted (and sometimes the congregation, too). She understands that no sermon ever does everything the preacher hopes it will do, but often does more than the preacher ever realizes or anticipates. In many cases, Sylvia has read and helped me think through the sermon before I actually preached it. In most cases, she has sat through the sermon twice each Sunday (a testament not just of her devotion, but also of her endurance). She talks to me about it before I preach it and after I preach it. She is watching people's reactions while I am preaching, and is listening to people's reactions when it is over. She is always pulling for me and praying for me while I am preaching, and she is my biggest encourager. Whenever I stand to preach, she is beside me.

And then, of course, there are the people who are before me when I preach — the congregation. While it is true that not all pastors are good preachers, and not all preachers are good pastors, it is also true that good pastoring makes preaching more effective. People have a higher tolerance for ineffective preaching on Sunday if the preacher has been a pastor to them through the week. If pastors have been holding congregants in the light throughout the week — visiting them, texting them, calling them, emailing them, and praying for them — the congregants will hear their pastors' sermons with more graceful eagerness than they would if their preachers were strangers to them. Moreover, preachers who love their people and share life with them have a pastoral sensitivity to the people in their congregations. Some preachers know the Bible, but not the people. Others know the people, but not the Bible. But the most effective preachers are those who know the truth about both and can communicate the truth in a credible way.

In the letter to the Romans, Paul asks the rhetorical question, "How shall they hear without a preacher?" But the reverse of that question is also a valid way of considering the ministry of preaching: How can anyone preach without hearers? In every church I have ever served, there have been different types of hearers. As in the parable Jesus told, when the seed of God's word is planted, every type of soil has been represented: the hardened path where the seed is immediately snatched away, the rocky ground where the seed does not take root, and the thorny field where the seed is choked out by other factors that compete with the word. But thankfully, there is the good soil in which the seed takes root and bears fruit. I am so thankful for the people in every congregation I have ever served who never heard a bad sermon, or when they did, they didn't tell me. They were always ready and receptive, hungry for a word from God. It is amazing how the people who long to hear a word from the Lord always seem to hear it through the preacher, and sometimes in spite of the preacher. It is often the case that individuals in the congregation hear something different, and many times they hear something the preacher didn't say. Because of my insecurities as a preacher, I do not think I could have faced a congregation Sunday after Sunday if it were not for my assurance that there were going to be people in that congregation who would hear a word from God through my preaching whether the sermon was good or not. And, in fact, most of the sermons in this book are included in this book because of the gracious people of Earle Street Baptist Church, who suggested that I include them.

I have never preached alone. There have always been people who have stood behind me, beside me, and before me.

Touchstones of My Preaching

The longer preachers preach, the more they repeat themselves. In my preaching, I find myself repeating some thoughts over and over. In most cases, I can trace these themes back to individuals. In some cases, I know the quotations are not original with me, but I cannot trace them back to their original source. And in a few cases, the statements may have originated with me (but I doubt it).

The truth will make you mad before it makes you free.[46]

The desire to please God pleases God. — Marshall Sargent

Give as much of yourself as you know how to as much of Jesus as you can understand. — Ansel McGill, who may have gotten it from another source

God is not an enemy whose favor you must win, but a friend whose grace you can trust.[47] — Chuck Poole

You cannot change anyone, but God can change you. — Ansel McGill

---

46 Otis Moss, Jr, "The Black Church Revolution," in *The Black Christian Experience*, ed. Emmanuel L. McCall (Nashville: Broadman Press, 1972), 103.
47 Charles E. Poole. *Don't Cry Past Tuesday: Hopeful Words for Difficult Days* (Macon, Georgia: Smyth and Helwys Publishing, Inc., 1991), 22.

Sometimes God does less than we hope, but God is always doing more than we know.[48] — Chuck Poole

Take the high road and the long view.

The problem with most of us is not that we are empty and need to be filled, but that we are filled and need to be emptied. — Loyd Melton

The biggest hindrance in our witness is not that our message is unbelievable, but that we are unbelievable. — Loyd Melton

Sometimes the way God answers our prayers is by changing our prayers. — Marshall Sargent

When we are waiting, we are not doing nothing. We are doing the most important something we can do. We are allowing our souls to grow up.[49] — Sue Monk Kidd, quoting an unnamed monk

When we try to do everything, we end up doing nothing.

Faith is not a place to stand, but a path on which to walk. — Source unknown

The word of God comforts the disturbed and disturbs the comfortable. — Source unknown

---

48 Charles E. Poole. *Beyond the Broken Lights: Simple Words at Sacred Edges* (Macon, Georgia: Smyth and Helwys Publishing, Inc. 2000.
49 Sue Monk Kidd, *When the Heart Waits: Spiritual Direction for Life's Sacred Questions* (San Francisco, 1992), 22-23.

A good sermon should warm the heart, challenge the mind, and tan the hide. — Ansel McGill

Sorrow has a way of coming down every street and knocking on every door. — Ansel McGill

We should whisper when the Lord whispers, and shout when the Lord shouts. — John Roy, quoting his professor

Sometimes we are judged not so much for our sins, but by our sins. — Ansel McGill

God's love will see the world to sleep. In life, it will bear us up. In death, it will pillow our heads in perfect peace. And in the kingdom beyond death, it will disclose in perfections beyond our conceiving, all we have hoped and feared to see.[50] — Theron Price

Do what you can. Because when you've done what you can, you've done what you should.[51] — Chuck Poole

Lord, You know our hearts. Help us to know Yours.

Yesterday is a canceled check. Tomorrow is a promissory note. But today is ready cash. — Jim Wooten

---

50 Theron Price. *Faith, Hope, and Love* (a booklet of meditations presented during a retreat at Lake Junaluska, September, 1980).
51 Charles E. Poole. *Is Life Fair? God's Words for Hard Times* (Macon, Georgia: Smyth and Helwys, Publishing, Inc., 1996), 64.

We are sinners saved by grace. The sin is our own; the grace is a gift from God. — Ansel McGill

The church is better and worse than its critics know it to be. — Ansel McGill

CPSIA information can be obtained
at www.ICGtesting.com
Printed in the USA
BVHW031046271022
650468BV00015B/465